The Perfect Close:
The Secret To Closing Sales

The Best-Selling Practices & Techniques
For Closing The Deal

James Muir

Best Practice International

THE PERFECT CLOSE
© April 2016
By JAMES MUIR

Best Practice International
14267 Bailey Hill Way
Herriman, UT 84096
http://www.bestpracticeinternational.com/

Ordering Information:
Quantity sales. Special discounts are available on quantity purchases by corporations, associations, and others. For details, contact the publisher at the address above.

For information visit http://PureMuir.com

Book Cover design by Ivan Terzic

Publisher Best Practice International

ISBN 978-0692689103
BISAC: Business & Economics / Sales & Selling / General
1. Business & Economics 2. Sales & Selling 3. General
First Edition: April 2016

Dedication

*To Mahan Khalsa - For teaching me that intent counts
more than technique.*

Table of Contents

Free Additional Resources

I t was impossible to include everything in the book and still keep it to a manageable size. So I've created a place for you where you can download free resources that will help you further your sales journey.

You can download these resources at PureMuir.com/resources. There you will find illustrations, special reports, mind maps, checklists, forms for research and planning meetings, sample agendas, guides to make some of the exercises in the book easier, and more.

I will continue to add to these resources as time goes on. I hope you find them valuable as you continue to expand your skills and knowledge.

Why I Wrote This Book

Early in my sales career I struggled with closing because I came from the services part of the business where we delivered the services that clients were buying. During this time I never appreciated all the challenges with being in sales because the process by which prospects became clients was hidden to me.

Eventually, I became a technical resource to help the sales force during their presentations. This position provided me a ringside seat to observe all of the sales processes and scenarios involved in interacting with prospective clients. It was a big eye opener for me. I came to really admire the sellers. Great salespeople are amazing. They are creators—generating something out of nothing. They are the key catalyst for positive change for not only their customers but also the companies for which they work. They are the spark that makes everything happen. They are both openers and closers.

I remember thinking how hard it looked. I was grateful for not having to do those functions and recall saying to myself, "I hope I never have to do that."

Sure enough, circumstances changed in a way that required I become a field sales person. I was faced front and center with performing those same functions I had hoped I'd never have to do. Despite my anxiety I had a great deal of enthusiasm. Unfortunately I didn't know where to channel my energy or where to go to learn what I didn't know. I developed an appreciation for new and inexperienced salespeople because that's exactly what I was—new and inexperienced.

In my circle of newbie salespeople, I struggled. I had no models to emulate. I had no training I could go through; no immediate resources I could tap. So, I turned to books.

For many years, I read every sales training book I could find. The books were helpful—some more than others—and I became an expert on one technique and then another. My tenacity and education paid off as I began to receive larger and larger commission checks. Yet, for me, something was missing. Regardless of all the time and effort I'd invested in my career, I still wasn't completely comfortable with my process.

After many years of considerable success in field sales I was asked to manage. As a sales manager, I worked with various professionals (some in field sales, some not). Many of these folks were top-tier professionals in their given domains who would be called upon to assist others in a selling effort (like I did early in my career). And sometimes, despite not being in sales, they would be called upon to go in solo to support the sales effort. Almost all of these professionals at one time or another confessed to me that they just didn't know what to say or do at the end of a call or meeting in order to "close the sale." They admitted that they found closing uncomfortable and the least favorite part of their job.

The lion's share of these individuals admitted that rather than moving the process forward with intention, they would just keep talking or presenting until they ran out of time—praying that their prospects would ask *them* for the business. I found this to be a common challenge with my field reps, as well.

Their frustration resonated with me because this was my exact experience. Ironically, sometimes it worked. My clients would be so "sold" (over-sold really) that they would literally interrupt me (because time was running short) and proceed to close me on the next step. Let me illustrate with an example from earlier in my career.

Because I came from the service side of the business, one of the first things I did as a new sales person was to diagram all the steps that I expected a customer to go through when evaluating solutions. There were twelve steps and next to each I indicated whether it was the customer's responsibility or my responsibility. I turned this into a form that I shared with my prospects during discovery (yeah, you just figured out how anal-retentive I was back then).

While presenting to one particular business I found things were going very well. Rapport, need, and understanding of how the solution would benefit them were all present. I could tell the key decision maker and his staff were on board. Yet, in my exuberance I didn't stop selling and close. I just kept right on going. It's crazy because I could see they were ready. Nevertheless, I found myself launching into even more details of my solution.

Finally, as our time together crept past two hours, the top executive interrupted me mid-sentence, "James!" Rotating and sliding my 12-step form toward me, he pointed to a box near the bottom where I'd typed "Deliver Agreement," and he said, "I'm right here in your process."

Embarrassed and red faced, I apologized, and then we discussed the agreement.

At the end of our conversation he told me, "At first I was wondering when you would ask me to buy. Then I realized that you weren't going to. You were never going to stop. I HAD to interrupt you. We were already over time. Not everyone would do that, you know."

I found myself reflecting on this over and over again. "Why didn't I ask?" I thought. Why did I keep going when I knew the time was right? In the end I determined that it was because I was uncomfortable and didn't know the right words to say. This introspection of my discomfort in closing the sale led my curious mind to studying the psychology and physiology (the science) involved in both asking for and committing others to a final decision. The result of this exploration is *The Perfect Close*.

Why did I write this book? I wrote it for all the sales and service professionals who are like I was—lacking a clear and simple way to bring sales to closure. I want you to enjoy the same success and enjoyment that I experienced once I discovered that there IS a natural way to ask for commitment that is superior to the standard techniques out there. You don't have to change your personality or become someone you're not, and it's flexible enough to use at every given stage. It eliminated all of the stress, tension, and uncertainty I felt when it came time to close. It's a way of asking that made my prospective clients see me as both a facilitator and consultant.

Certainly, there is more to successful selling than just closing, however, for those struggling to find a clear and simple way to ask for commitment, this book may be the single most-valuable learning activity you can do for yourself. If you are simply ready to hone your selling game and take it to the next level, you now have in your hands the best practice for closing and advancing the sale.

If you invest the short amount of time it takes to learn this clear and simple method, you will dramatically improve your sales results and make all of your interactions profoundly more enjoyable.

It is my hope that you will achieve the same level of success and happiness that knowing these things has afforded me.

Introduction

D id you know there is a method to closing that is nearly always successful (in the 95% range), is zero pressure for you and your client, and involves just two questions? It's true. This book outlines the method. Even better, you can learn it in as little as five minutes.

It doesn't require that you change your personality or become someone you're not, and it's flexible enough to use on every kind of sale at every given stage.

It eliminates all of the stress and tension that some professionals feel when it comes to asking for commitments, and because it's facilitative, it completely eliminates the negative connotation many people associate with sales.

It makes clients feel more educated, in control, and causes them to see you as a facilitator and consultant.

I call it *The Perfect Close*, and if you'd like to cut to the chase and learn it right now, jump to Chapter 12. You'll have the technique before the end of the chapter.

The rest of this book will help you maximize The Perfect Close technique as well as all of your face-to-face client encounters. It will share cutting-edge psychology that explains why The Perfect Close works, and why your intent matters more than the technique.

You'll discover how to add value to every single meeting you have, and how to plan your meetings in a way that differentiates you from your competition.

You'll learn to add continuous momentum and advance your sales in a way that ultimately culminates in more closed business and faster closed business.

All this you will learn while you move toward a Zen-like state where closing is effortless and in full alignment with your personal values.

The bottom line is you will know everything necessary to close every sale. You don't need a hundred-and-one closes (one for every occasion), and you don't even need to master selling. All you really need is an easy, facilitative way to advance your sales to closure. It's that simple.

You can download a PDF model of The Perfect Close right now at PureMuir.com as a reference guide. Throughout the book I mention resources I've made available for you at PureMuir.com. Go there! Please, use them! This book and the tools I've provided to support you offer the best of everything I have researched, seen, and put into practice myself in the realm of closing. It is THE best practice in sales closing all in one, life-changing, little book. And, it is simple to boot! Let's get started!

CHAPTER 1

Why Should I Bother to Learn The Perfect Close?

"Being pushy, isn't part of my nature. I hate pitching. I detest anything that smacks of manipulation."

–Jill Konrath

Professionals sell about half of what they set out to sell. For a decade or more, quota attainment by professional sales reps has hovered between 50% to 60%, and most recently quota attainment has been trending downward.[1] Some industries are slightly better, many are much worse, and sales as a profession continues to be among the highest turnover positions in business.[2]

So what's going on here? There are a host of reasons for these dynamics: economic challenges, increased competition, time constraints, pricing pressures and lower margins, increased complexity, increased market noise, challenges servicing existing clients, dysfunctional buying and selling, and the list goes on.

The face of selling and the way customers buy has been undergoing a fundamental change for years. Josh Gordon, author of *Selling 2.0,* and others began to document this trend back in 2000. The maturation of the Internet has forever changed the way that the business-to-business and business-to-consumer buying process takes place.

Older methods of selling continue to wane in effectiveness. Tom Snyder coauthor of *Escaping the Price-Driven Sale* says it this way, "The key to value creation is providing insight rather than information. In today's marketplace customer value does not reside in flogging products or services but rather the manner in which products and services are sold."[3]

A consistent set of individuals across all industries and professions are embracing this change, and in spite of the above-mentioned challenges they continue to outperform regardless of the circumstances. In the coming chapters, we will explore exactly why certain individuals not only succeed but actually thrive in these conditions. Understanding and adopting their successful habits will give you an edge as you ultimately implement The Perfect Close.

So back to the original question—why should you take the time to learn The Perfect Close? Well, the most fundamental reason would be to generate more sales and earn more revenue, but that's just scratching the surface. Let me outline why you will find it worth your time to learn *this particular approach* as the vehicle to drive your closing process.

First, it is very easy to learn. You can learn the basic approach in less than five minutes. Actually, it is extremely important that the approach *be* simple, which leads me to...

Are Closing Techniques Like Diets?

I am a fitness buff, and unless you've been living under a rock for the past 30 years you know that there are countless diets and other dietary or nutritional products promising all kinds of miraculous results. Over the years, in my quest for better and better fitness, I have learned (and tried) many of these diet and fitness solutions. It has now become a hobby to analyze each new diet, gadget, and technique to understand their underpinnings and how much truth, practicality, and hype exist in each.

Unfortunately, a huge percentage of these products are garbage. Many of them have an idea or principle that is valid, but the results are blown way out of proportion in relation to what can truly be achieved using these solutions. On the other hand, some actually work...

Take diets for example, there are quite a number of them with merit. The problem is that some diets are ridiculously complicated and too difficult to maintain, let alone adopt as an ongoing lifestyle. All the current leaders in fitness and nutrition now agree that the ease of going on and maintaining a diet is a major factor (if not *the* major factor) in the creation of a successful diet. If people can't effectively start or maintain the diet, it doesn't matter how effective it *could* be because they won't be able to sustain it. And that, my friends, is why I am going on and on about diets in a book about advancing the sale—because closing techniques suffer similar complications.

Name any book on closing, and odds are, I've read it. There are books with hundreds of sales closes in them, each with their own clever name, like the *board of nails* close, or the *one-dollar-for-one-hundred-dollars* close, or my all-time favorite the *Atomic-what-would-Jesus-do-BOMB* close (no, I'm not kidding). Someday, to give you a good laugh and protect the innocent souls out there who might actually consider using one of these gems, I'll put up a website with a Sales Closing Wall of Shame listing all of the ridiculous closes I've collected over the years.

Just like the diets, most of these closes are garbage—and by garbage, I mean counter-productive. They will actually *hurt* your chances of closing the sale (in upcoming chapters, I will share well-researched studies in this area), but also like the diets, some of these techniques actually work from time to time. And thus, the confusion sets in.

Some of these old-school closes are very elaborate, are specialized for particular situations, and require intricate setups. Some take hours to execute. This is again where they are like diets. If there is too much to remember, or they are too complicated to execute, then no one will use them. Who wants to take the time to memorize one-hundred-and-one closes—one for every possible situation? What if in the heat of the moment I use the wrong one? Oh, the pressure!

It's a waste of time and effort to use what amounts to a counter-productive close 90% of the time. It is also totally unnecessary. Again, just like a diet, the approach must be easy enough to follow so that when it comes time to actually use the approach, it becomes second nature.

This is one of the reasons why you should learn The Perfect Close—because it is simple, easy to learn, and you can use it in every situation. It's so effective, in fact, that I guarantee you will use it in all sorts of non-selling situations as well.

But Is It Really Perfect?

I can hear some of you now, "James, you have a lot of chutzpah calling this The Perfect Close. Sure, being easy to learn and easy to use is good, but that doesn't make it *perfect.*"

I agree completely. We could round up a bunch of closes that are easy to learn and use but are completely ineffective and/or even counter-productive. If The Perfect Close were nothing more than easy to learn and use, in my mind it would not qualify as *perfect.* But The Perfect Close is so much more for you than just easy to learn and use. Here's a few more reasons why.

Tricks & Manipulation Techniques Don't Work

Now is probably a good time to mention that I generally hate sales tricks and manipulative techniques. Like my friend Jill Konrath (who is a tremendous author, teacher, and inspiration), I hate anything designed to trap or manipulate people. In fact, I don't even like the term *perfect close*. I prefer to think of it as an *approach* as opposed to a *close*, but I had to call it something. So I took the advice of one of my students who called it *perfect* (besides, The Perfect *Approach* sounds a little funky to me).

As we will cover in an upcoming chapter, your intent when working with a client matters a great deal and is the foundation of the entire approach. Genuine, honest intent leaves zero room for trickery and manipulation.

What else could possibly qualify this approach as perfect? Well, brace yourself—it nearly always works. Yes, along the lines of 95%.

Oh, I can hear the cries now, "You mean to tell me, James, that every time I use this approach I'm going to get a contract and a sale?!" No, that's not what I mean (though many times you will indeed get a sale). Allow me to explain.

How Science Has Advanced Selling—What We Now Know

The world (and especially the sales world) owes a great debt of gratitude to a man named Neil Rackham who conducted the largest-ever study of professional selling—observing more than 35,000 sales calls in over 20 countries. Rackham's studies have illuminated many important dynamics regarding selling, and we will be referring to him and his studies' results throughout this work. Among other things, Rackham introduced and labeled the sales concept of the *advance*.

In his seminal work *SPIN Selling*, Rackham defines an advance as an event that takes place, either during the call or right after it that moves the sale toward a decision.[4] I will add additional important nuance to this in an upcoming chapter. For now, how this relates to The Perfect Close is this: If The Perfect Close doesn't produce a sale or contract, it will always produce an advance. Or said another way, The Perfect Close will either produce an actual close, or it will move the sale toward a decision—every time.

Let me tell you from personal experience that this is a wonderful quality because it means that the approach can be used over and over again, each time advancing the sale toward ultimate closure. Because the approach produces either a close or an advance, in that sense, it always works. That is an incredible advantage over every other method.

Are You Making the Same Mistake Over and Over?

I know what you're thinking. Did he just say "over and over" in that last paragraph? Are you afraid that the approach will require that you ask for the sale over and over? Are you worried that you will be seen as too aggressive or pushy by repeatedly asking for business? Well, you should be.

Your instincts serve you well here because one of the findings that Rackham discovered is that within the same call, past the first attempt, there is a *negative* correlation between the number of times a salesperson asks for a close and sales success. Additionally, he found that the more closing attempts there were past the first attempt on the same call the lower the success rate.[5] That's right, and this data has been widely published since 1988. So everything you've heard about the ABCs of selling meaning "Always Be Closing" is complete hogwash. Asking for the sale over and over will do nothing more than hurt your chances of actually closing.

We will expand on this topic in a later chapter. The takeaway here is that the inner instinct you have to not badger a client is correct. Asking for the sale more than once per meeting is counter-productive and will hurt your sales.

So what did I mean by "over and over?" I mean that once you learn it, the approach is flexible enough to use over and over without offending clients, and without you sounding like a broken record. I would also say that while it is possible to get more than one advance in each meeting with a client (more on that later), generally you will be using the approach only once per encounter with the client.

Do Real Closers Have Schizophrenia?

In this same vein, as a sales manager I have coached sales reps for years, and one of the comments I often hear is, "After I've worked to develop a good relationship with a client, I have a hard time just suddenly changing my personality into Mr. Aggressive Super-Closer and going for the jugular because 'corporate needs more sales now!'" This is also a common challenge among other non-selling professionals who must sell their own services.

One of my favorite things about The Perfect Close approach that makes it so *perfect* is that it doesn't require you to suddenly change your personality and become something you are not. You will see that it is totally natural and absolutely non-confrontational. This allows professionals and salespeople alike to close more business in a way that avoids the negative, slick salesperson association that is so often well-deserved among some individuals.

Because the approach is collaborative and non-confrontational it completely eliminates the tension and stress felt by both clients and professionals. Clients will see you as a valuable facilitator. The Perfect Close approach will set you apart and differentiate you from your competition and help you build long-lasting relationships that go beyond a simple transaction.

One of the reasons the approach creates better relationships is that clients feel more in control of the entire process. The approach puts them in the driver's seat while you guide them, and ironically, this accelerates the entire process because of the trust factor involved. As Stephen M. R. Covey has outlined so well in his book *The Speed of Trust*, "Trust always affects two outcomes: speed and cost. When trust goes down, speed goes down and cost goes up."[6] Of course the corollary to this is the focus of his book, which is that as we increase trust we both increase speed and decrease costs.

"Trust always affects two outcomes: speed and cost. When trust goes down, speed goes down and cost goes up." –Stephen M. R. Covey, The Speed of Trust

---

I have found this to be so true that occasionally clients over-trust to the point where they begin to take shortcuts. That is, they trust so much in the sales professional that they don't take the time to cover certain details because they are confident that they will ultimately be taken care of. This is valuable trust indeed and something that must be managed with great responsibility and care.

The benefit this brings is that it accelerates the entire process and maintains the momentum of the sale. You will cover more steps in less time, and spend less time between steps.

Are You Giving Your Clients What They Expect?

As you guide clients through each step of the sales process, you will be giving them more of what they expect—while at the same time improving their perception of your solution. This is because the client can see the entire picture, and the important major and minor steps are highlighted for what happens before, during, and after the sale.

All too often the salesperson presents their solution at a speed far in excess to the client's ability to absorb it—feeding them from the proverbial fire hose. This happens because the salesperson fears they may not get another chance to present all the glorious features and benefits of their solution. So, they fervently spew everything they can in whatever time is allotted.

While this rapid rate of transfer may make sense to the salesperson—who goes through this process day in and day out—it unfortunately backfires because clients frequently can't absorb information at this same rate.

The Perfect Close approach addresses this challenge by allowing the client to throttle each step to a rate they can receive and digest. This increases the value of each step and of the client's overall perception of your solution.

One interesting aspect of the approach worth mentioning is that, while not ideal, it can often step you through what to do next during a client encounter without you even realizing what the most appropriate next step is. Of course it is always better for you to know your own process, but this aspect of the approach is nice for new or inexperienced professionals who may not have yet determined their sales process. In most cases, the approach will naturally advance you through all the steps and literally teach them to you on the fly.

A valuable side-effect of the approach is that your client's responses to each advance will tell you exactly where you stand with that client. As a sales manager, this is tremendous for accurate forecasting. It also allows us to quickly identify prospects that will never close and eliminates surprises where clients suddenly go with a competitor.

If you have ever despised manipulative selling techniques or even disliked the confrontation associated with closing, you are likely to see advancing the sale in an entirely different light after reading *The Perfect Close*. You won't see advancing the sale or closing as something you do

TO the client, but rather you'll see it as something you do WITH the client—collaborating with the client to continually advance them toward their desired results.

Let's quickly summarize the five top reasons why it makes sense to learn The Perfect Close:

All of this is much more fun than the high-pressure, confrontational approach of yesterday. Picture it—having fun with clients, working on the same side of the table with them, helping them achieve better results while achieving better results yourself—all with a repeatable process that will serve you your entire life. That is how it works.

Are you ready to get started?

Closing Secret #1 - *Closing is more effective when it isn't high-pressure or manipulative.*

Closing Secret #2 - *The best closing approach must be easy enough to follow so that when it comes time to actually use the approach, it is second nature.*

Note: There are 22 Closing Secrets referenced throughout this book. Download the reference guide along with a PDF model of The Perfect Close at <u>PureMuir.com</u>

CHAPTER 2

What Is Closing Anyway?

"Closing is the act of obtaining commitments, including all of the decisions that advance the sale."

–Anthony Iannarino

So what exactly is closing? There are nearly as many definitions as there are authors, trainers, and salespeople. Some of these definitions are quite good. Others—not so much. For example, "Doing whatever you have to do to get the customer to sign," isn't so good in my book.

Asking for the sale, asking for the order, and similar definitions are common. This type of definition essentially boils down to "that thing you say that gets the customer to buy." While useful for some purposes, this definition perpetuates one of the biggest problems with closing techniques—that it paints the close as an all or nothing request. And as we shall see below, the vast majority of sales cannot be treated this way.

Other definitions are much more broad and holistic. These definitions boil down to something like, "Closing is everything you do from the beginning of the sale to final completion of the transaction and beyond." And I believe this, by the way. The problem is that these types of definitions essentially redefine *closing* as all of *selling*, which makes the definition so broad that it limits its usefulness. And we're only defining this so we can get better results, right?

There really is no reason for us to re-invent the wheel here. For our purposes in this book we are going to accept Neil Rackham's definition of a *close* (just like we did for the term *advance*) and build on it. Here is Rackham's definition: "A close is anything that puts the customer in a position involving some kind of commitment."[1]

> *"A close is anything that puts the customer in a position involving some kind of commitment."* –Neil Rackham

This gives us a workable definition that fits somewhere between "it's all or nothing" and "it's everything." This is an important aspect of The Perfect Close because while we will sometimes get a final completed transaction, many times what we will achieve is an advance. For the most part, I use the term *close* and *advance* synonymously. That will allow us to discuss the idea of "closing on a minor-step," "going for a minor-close," "advancing the sale," or "getting an advance." All of these essentially mean the same thing.

Do You Have Any of the Common Misconceptions About Closing?

Common Misconceptions About Closing

1. Closing techniques work (i.e., they are effective).
2. Closing more frequently works (i.e., asking more frequently for the business is effective).
3. Closing techniques work on all kinds of sales, large or small.
4. Closing techniques show you want the business (clients see gambits as willingness to do business).
5. Clients are happier once they've made a decision, & closing techniques help them do that.
6. If you do everything else right, closing will happen by itself.

Misconception #1 - Closing Gambits Work

Some people call these "techniques." I call them gambits—a contrived or manipulative phrase designed to force a commitment. Some folks believe there is a magic phrase that if you say it, it will cause your client to be overcome with your verbal persuasion and buy whatever it is you are selling.

The premise behind virtually all of the advice on closing techniques is that it is effective to use these gambits when making an effort to close business. People who have a lot of faith in closing techniques might be surprised to discover that Rackham tested the correlation between a favorable attitude toward closing techniques and actual sales results. He found that individuals with the best attitude toward closing techniques were actually less likely to hit their sales targets. In the study, test subjects with a *favorable attitude* toward closing techniques actually performed 21% below those with *less favorable* attitudes.[2]

In a later study of the effectiveness of sales-closing training, Rackham tested whether or not salespeople utilized closing techniques more frequently after having received training on the subject, and to what degree closing techniques increased sales success. Rackham states the results this way, "Closing [as a technique] turned out to be negatively related to success. After the training, the sellers used more closing techniques—so in one sense the training was effective. However, because fewer calls succeeded, the overall effect of the training was a decrease in sales." In the study the overall success rate decreased sales success by approximately 15%.[3]

So yes, closing gambits work—at losing you business.

Misconception #2 - Closing More Often Works

Thanks to Alec Baldwin in the movie *Glengarry Glen Ross* we all know the ABCs of sales: "Always Be Closing." We also sometimes hear this as the axiom, "Close early and often." Unfortunately, as alluded to previously, this has been tested, and beyond the first attempt there is a negative correlation between closing frequency and sales call success. In his first study on the topic Rackham found that *high close calls* (calls that averaged 5.8 closing behaviors) had a success rate of approximately 37%; where *low close calls* (calls that averaged 1.4 closing behaviors) had a success rate of approximately 70%. So, increasing close attempts actually proved to be 33% less effective.

Success on High vs. Low-close calls

Success Rate

33% More Effective

High-Close   Low-Close

Misconception #3 - Closing Techniques Work on All Kinds of Sales

Proponents of closing gambits would have you believe that these approaches can be applied effectively across a wide spectrum of sales—everything from rocket wreckage to everlasting Gobstoppers. Unfortunately, research suggests otherwise.

Neil Rackham discovered in his research that closing techniques *can indeed* be more effective when the scope of the sale is *small*. The three metrics of the study were:

> Transaction Time – How long did each sale or attempted sale take?

> Number of Closes – How often did the seller use a closing behavior?

> Percentage of Sale – What percent of transactions resulted in a purchase?

What the study found is that when the value of the goods being sold was small, use of closing techniques both speeded the transaction time as well as the number of transactions resulting in a sale. In *low-close* calls where the number of closes averaged 1.3 attempts per transaction, transactions had a success ratio of 72%. In *high-close* calls where the number of attempts per call averaged 1.9, transactions had a success ratio of 76%.[4] So in selling low-value goods, more attempts to close improved performance by 4%.

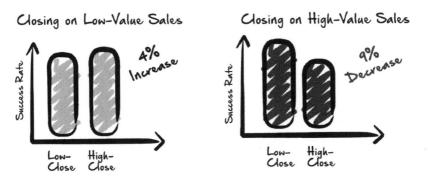

However, as the value of the goods being sold increased, success in the transaction reversed and closing became counter-productive. In the case of the higher-value goods in *low-close* calls where the number of closes averaged 2.7 attempts per transaction, transactions had a success ratio of 42%. In *high-close* calls where the number of attempts per call averaged 4.5, transactions had a success ratio of 33%.[5]

So while attempts were up and transaction time was speeded, overall success dropped measurably in the high-value goods arena.

Rackham describes the phenomenon, "The psychological effect of pressure seems to be this. If I'm asking you to make a very small decision, then—if I pressure—it's easier for you to say yes than to have an argument. Consequently, with a small decision, the effect of pressure is positive. But this isn't so with large decisions. The bigger the decision, the more negatively people generally react to pressure."[6]

Rackham observes, "By forcing the customer into a decision, closing techniques speed the sales transaction." And that, "Closing techniques may increase the chances of making a sale with low-priced products. With expensive products or services, they reduce the chances of making a sale."[7]

This is an important dynamic to be aware of when planning your efforts to close sales.

So what is the threshold? At what price point do closing techniques become counter-productive? In Rackham's study it was only $109.[8]

While your situation may be different, all of the people I work with sell goods and services with values higher than this level. So if you are selling a lot of stuff lower than $109, maybe now is the time to whip out the *Double-Reverse Close*. On the other hand, if your solutions are somewhere north of this, the idea that using closing gambits is effective is not only wrong—it is counter-productive and will sabotage your closing efforts.

Misconception #4 - Closing Techniques Show You Want the Business

At face value this is completely true. Why would a person bother trying to close the sale if they didn't actually want it? This isn't really the issue. The client knows you want the business. The real question here is whether or not your use of a closing gambit is seen positively or negatively by the client.

In a study conducted by Jon Hawes, James Strong, and Bernard Winick, 237 industrial buyers were questioned on this subject. Six closure techniques were researched: The Assumptive Close, Yes Set, Model/Example, Reciprocity, If-Then, and Impending Event. The customer's trust in the salesperson was then tested by a means of 24 pairs of characteristics on a seven-step scale. The results showed that every single technique tested damaged the basis of trust. Predictably, the most manipulative techniques damaged trust the most.[9]

If you want to show your client you want their business—tell them. Or, do something special for them. There are far better ways to show you want the business than insulting them with a closing gambit.

Misconception #5 - Clients Are Happier After They've Made a Decision (so using closing techniques on them is actually helping them)

Let me rephrase this. The thinking seems to be: Clients are happier after they have made a decision, so manipulating or pressuring the client into a purchase is actually for their own good.

I'm sure you recognize this as the-end-justifies-the-means thinking, and I'm sure it makes for great rationalization among some salespeople. But, as it turns out, it is wrong. How satisfied people are with their decisions after they make them while under pressure happens to be an area well studied by social scientists. The studies show that the vast majority of people are very much *less satisfied* with the decisions they make under pressure.[10-13] This is especially true with purchasing decisions. This can have serious negative ramifications to your after-the-sale relationships and long-term success with clients. If you want to avoid buyer remorse, cancelations, and left-field complaints after the sale I recommend you avoid this thinking.

Let's sum up the first five misconceptions and what we can learn from them before moving on to our final misconception.

Common Misconceptions About Closing	Lesson Learned
1. Closing techniques work (i.e., they are effective).	– Use of closing techniques has been shown to be negatively correlated to sales success when used frequently.
2. Closing more frequently works (i.e., asking more frequently for the business is effective).	– Past the first attempt, there is a negative correlation between closing and sales success.
3. Closing techniques work on all kinds of sales, large or small.	– Increasing closing frequency is modestly more effective in small purchases. – Increasing closing frequency is less effective in larger purchases. – Increasing closing frequency reduces transaction time (win or lose) regardless of size.
4. Closing techniques show you want the business (clients see gambits as willingness to do business).	– Use of traditional closing techniques reduces client trust.
5. Clients are happier once they've made a decision, & closing techniques help them do that.	– Clients are less satisfied with decisions when forced to make them under pressure.

These are important dynamics to remember as we plan our closing approach. Now, let's move on to misconception #6.

Misconception #6 - If You Do Everything Else Right, the Sale Will Close Itself

With all this talk of how closing techniques and gambits don't work you might come to the conclusion that you should make no closing attempt at all. Indeed, there are several proponents of this mentality. But alas, this is taking it too far. Studies show that you *must* make an effort to advance the sale in order to be successful. Let us look at the data.

Across all industries, studies show that the problem of not advancing the sale *at all* is much bigger than the problem of using closing gambits. While it varies per industry, surveys indicate that the percentage of salespeople and professionals who never ask for a commitment or an advance ranges from 50% to 90%. The average across industries seems to be about 60%.[14-18]

50%-90% of salespeople never ask for commitment

Based on research done by Huthwaite, asking at least one closing question will raise your chances of advancing or closing the sale by 36% or so. One study showed that asking just one closing question raised the percentage of successful sales from 25% to 61%.[19]

36% ⬆ Increase

Rackham says it this way, "Traditional closing techniques are not the best way to obtain commitment from a customer in a major sale. But... as we've seen, doing nothing isn't effective either. The sale doesn't close itself."[20]

This is an important point. You *must* make some sort of effort to advance or close the sale. The sale will not close itself.

In a related area (again it varies across industries), a large percentage of deals are lost to no decision. That is, business is not lost to a competitor, but rather the client decides to do nothing. In many industries it is the single largest reason for the loss of sales. The percentage of losses due to no decision ranges from 20% to 80% depending on industry with the average seeming to be around 45% to 60%.[21-24]

Approximately 50% of all sales are lost to no decision

Closing Secret #3 - You will have to make an effort to close the sale. The sale will not close itself. By asking for commitment in the right way you can move forward without being pushy.

According to social scientists using the Meyer-Briggs Type Indicator and other profiling systems, up to 41% of society are what they refer to as *options people* or people who are generally more comfortable before making a decision rather than after. They see non-decision as leaving them with options as opposed to making a decision which they see as limiting their choices.[25]

How you frame and communicate your offering matters a good deal to this population segment, but that isn't the focus of this book. The important takeaway is that part of your role is that of a facilitator—helping buyers come to a conclusion that is in their best interest.

Salespeople and professionals are frequently frustrated by *options people* because their decision process can take what seems like forever. This is one more reason why it is critical to be able to advance the sale in a non-manipulative way.

Why Traditional Closing Efforts Fail

There two main reasons why closing efforts fail.

1. Salespeople and professionals don't really make an effort.

2. When an effort is made, the approach used doesn't work (or is counter-productive).

In management parlance we refer to these as *will* and *skill*. That is, it's common that they either don't have the *will* to ask for a commitment, or they don't have the *skill* to ask for a commitment.

Of these two, managers prefer to see skill as the main problem because it is usually remedied through training. On the other hand, *will* or a reluctance to initiate the skill is seen by most managers as a much bigger challenge because it makes the skill irrelevant. In fact, many managers are of the opinion that *will* issues cannot be corrected. They argue that while a skill can be trained, reluctance to initiate a skill is a motivational issue and a personality attribute which cannot be learned.

I disagree. In my experience, the key to addressing any kind of reluctance is to address the underlying issues and beliefs that are the source of the reluctance. A paradigm shift in these underlying issues can make the reluctance disappear.

When it comes specifically to closing business I have discovered that reluctance is a symptom of fear and/or shame:

- The professional fears being pushy.

- The professional fears being humiliated.

- The professional fears being under-prepared.

- The professional fears losing a closed sale.

- The professional is ashamed to be in sales.

What you're about to discover is that The Perfect Close addresses four (and sometimes all five) of these underlying issues. This means that The Perfect Close is the solution to both the *will* challenge as well as the *skill* challenge.

By placing a little thought into the specific way we engage clients (the way we ask), we can move forward without being pushy. By crafting our questions in a way that makes replies predictable, we eliminate risk of humiliation. By keeping our questions simple and facilitative, there is no need to over-prepare. By using an ingeniously designed query, each reply will advance the sale. And perhaps most importantly, by selling with pure intent, sales becomes a noble profession not worthy of shame.

The Perfect Close will teach you the *skill* you need—exactly what to say. Once you discover how it aligns with your own value system it will help you with your *will* as well.

One more note on developing your desire. Zig Ziglar was fond of saying, "You can have everything in life that you want, if you will just help enough other people get what they want." Closing is an act of service. Ask yourself who you are closing for. Is it for you, or is it for them? What are your motives? I assure you, your customers can tell.

Making money is a wonderful side effect of closing well. But life is about more than making money; it's about making a difference in the lives of others.

Your customers expect you to help them make the positive changes that will bring about their desired results. They expect you to encourage them to become better than they are. Coaching customers toward improvement is a noble purpose. Accept the challenge. Be their coach and guide them through each little commitment it takes to achieve their goals.

Show them the way. Show them that each commitment is a step in the right direction. Encourage and challenge them to take action. When your clients achieve their goals, they will be grateful and thankful, and will credit you as a contributor to their success. This is the sweet spot of selling. Skills and technique are still very important factors, however once you have adopted this attitude and mindset (which you can do today) you will find your selling work infinitely more satisfying.

In fact, your mindset and intent are an important part of what makes The Perfect Close work. You might be surprised to discover that top sales performers have a more pronounced sense of purpose and outperform their peers who focus primarily on sales goals and money.[26]

For that reason I devote the next chapter to mindset and intent, and how to develop it within yourself. I think you will be surprised and fascinated by the new discoveries and science that has emerged in this area. What you are about to learn will help you with The Perfect Close as well as with all aspects of your personal life.

Closing Secret #4 - Understanding that closing is helping your client and in alignment with your personal values can eliminate reluctance.

Conclusion

Helping you discover and implement a successful approach to advancing and closing your sales is the purpose of this book. In the next chapter, we will make sure that our head is in the right place and get into the actual approach that you and your clients will find *perfect.*

CHAPTER 3

Adopting the Right Mindset

"If your intention is flawed, the best technique in the world will not save you."

–Jeff Shore

A
sk yourself, "Why do I want to advance this sale? Why do I want to close?" Actually think about it. What is driving your desire to move this opportunity forward?

As you think of the reasons, list them on a piece of paper. Most people will have less than five real reasons or drivers. Give it a shot—I promise this quick exercise will pay off.

Now, look at your list. Which one would you say is your top driver? Which is secondary and so on? Quickly prioritize them by what is motivating you the most.

Now complete the following sentence by inserting each of your motivations:

"Thanks for meeting with me today. My top priority is to [fill in the blank with your response]."

Try it for each of the drivers you wrote down.

How did it turn out? Is this something you would be willing to say to a prospective client? Would any of the reasons/motivations you wrote down be appropriate to say to a prospective client? In most cases, probably not, but what you might find extremely alarming is:

You are already communicating these desires unintentionally.

And these messages can have a very big effect on your results. Going into a client interaction with the wrong mindset can negatively affect the outcome. Conversely, the right mindset will positively affect your outcome. And that is the object of this chapter—to help you adopt the mindset that will positively affect all of your interactions.

How Mindset Affects Your Interactions

In the 1990s an Italian neurophysiologist named Giacomo Rizzolatti made an amazing discovery. He and his team were researching brain function using monkeys as test subjects. The monkeys were being monitored by machines that registered their brain activity.

Giacomo Rizzolatti

The scientists would encourage the monkeys to do various activities by offering a reward—a peanut, a food they love. When a monkey receives and eats a peanut the pleasure centers of their brains light up like a Christmas tree.

One day, one of the researchers ate a peanut in front of one of the monkeys, and an amazing thing happened. The monkey's pleasure centers lit up, just as if the monkey had eaten the peanut himself.

This was an unexpected development, and after much more investigation Rizzolatti's research team discovered that both monkeys and humans have something called mirror neurons that mimic both the actions and emotions of those around them (simian or human).

Much research in the area of mirror neurons has been completed since that time, and through the miracle of Functional Magnetic Resonance Imaging (fMRI) modern science can now watch the brain's responses to stimuli in real time.

As it turns out, mirror neurons are involved in a tremendous number of psycho-social areas including: language, learning, self-awareness, and most importantly for our discussion—understanding intentions and empathy.

A key takeaway here is that we are an empathic species. When we see another living being experience an emotion such as happiness or sorrow, our mirror neurons cause us to experience that emotion along with them. There is a whole invisible level of communication going on.

Mirror neurons make it possible to understand another person's point of view, and just as importantly as we'll see in a moment, their intent. It is important for us to be aware of these distinctions so that we understand the involuntary messages that our prospective clients are receiving from us.

What Is Your Nonverbal Communication Saying?

You may be familiar with the TV series *Lie to Me* which aired from 2009 – 2011. It was inspired by the work of renowned psychologist Paul Ekman who served as a consultant to the show. In the series Dr. Cal Lightman and his team used their knowledge of body language and facial expressions to effectively act as human polygraph machines and uncover the truth for law enforcement, law firms, corporations, and individuals.

The results are both entertaining and educational. For example, in the pilot episode Lightman interviews a man who refuses to speak at all, yet Lightman is able to discern vital information by gauging the man's reactions to his verbal cues.

Ekman began his research into nonverbal communication in the mid-1950s and focused on developing techniques for actually measuring nonverbal communication. Through empirical research of the muscular movements that create facial expression, he discovered that human beings are capable of more than 10,000 facial expressions—3,000 of which are relevant to emotion.

Psychologist Paul Ekman

Thanks to Ekman, we understand *micro-expressions* as brief, involuntary human facial expressions derived from immediate, inner emotions. Micro-expressions occur most frequently in high-stakes situations where people have something to lose or gain. Micro-expressions also occur when a person is consciously trying to conceal signs of how they are feeling, or when they do not consciously know how they are feeling.[1-2] Unlike regular facial expressions, micro-expressions are very brief in duration, lasting only ⅕₅th to ¹/₁₅th of a second, and very difficult if not impossible to hide.[3]

These systems are constantly in play. Your autonomic system is continuously sending signals that reveal your intentions and emotions. And just as importantly, your subconscious and autonomic systems are working 24/7 reading the body language of others to decode their intentions and emotions.

"Your autonomic system is continuously sending signals that reveal your intentions and emotions."

It is a deciphering system to determine friend or foe, honesty or deception—to decide if you are on their side or not. Basic, simple detections like these might be described as intuition or a *gut reaction*, but what is critical to understand is that your intentions are very important in your interactions with others.

You also give out similar signals with your voice. This too is mostly an unconscious activity.[4] It's called *paralanguage* and is the part of verbal communication that changes meaning via volume, pitch, intonation, and prosody. Paralinguistic speech plays a very important role in human interactions because every spoken communication contains these non-lexical speech signals.

Unlike micro-expressions, individuals have greater control over paralanguage. In most cases attitudes are expressed intentionally while emotions are more often expressed unintentionally.[5] Thus, paralanguage, while important, is secondary to visual cues.[6] Nevertheless it is important to be aware of the non-lexical messages we may be sending via our volume, pitch, speed, and intonation.

Your prospective clients are consciously and unconsciously detecting your involuntary signals which ultimately develops their general impressions about you. I know what you're thinking, "James, how can I possibly control all of these things in my interactions with clients?"

Consciously, you can't. Evidence indicates all but the most unusual subjects (patients with special mental conditions, for example) are unable to control the myriad involuntary signals we continually transmit.[2]

Further, the ability to detect intention develops at a very early age—emerging in children as young as 18 months and sometimes even earlier.[7, 8] So, basically, we're all experts at reading other people's intentions.

The good news, and the point of this chapter, is that you don't have to worry about your micro-expressions or attempt to control them if you adopt the right mindset. With the right intentions all of these signals will automatically be working for you without you having to think about it. Your body will be sending all of the right messages naturally.

With the right mindset your body will:

- Form the right, positive micro-expressions

- Deliver the ideal tonality

- Express the emotions with which you want your prospective client to empathize

- Communicate the right intention to maximize trust and rapport

All of this will greatly improve both the experience and the outcomes of your interactions with others.

What Is the Right Mindset?

To know what the ideal mindset is, it's important to understand what happens from a psychological perspective in the first seconds of any interaction. Many things occur, but among the first is a determination as to whether the person we're encountering is friend or foe (i.e. do they intend good or ill). This is the basis for forming trust. Immediately following that, the brain ascertains whether the other person has the actual ability to enact those intentions. This is the basis for determining someone's competency.

In an effort to determine the attributes that have the greatest impact on interpersonal communication scientists have conducted a tremendous number of studies. And by all accounts with more than 200 attributes having been tested, the most important and dominate attributes can be placed into two categories: warmth and competence.[9]

For clarity let's briefly define the difference between attributes and traits. Simply put, an attribute is a quality something has. For example, "Her voice has a warm tone," describes an attribute of someone's voice.

In contrast, traits are general behavior tendencies that a particular attribute produces. For example, "Her warm voice makes her very considerate and approachable."

The warmth attribute displays traits related to perceived intent, friendliness, helpfulness, sincerity, trustworthiness, and morality. Whereas the competence attribute reflects traits that are related to perceived ability, intelligence, skill, creativity, and efficacy.[10]

Which attribute is most important? While both warmth and competence consistently rise to the top of attributes in all studies, evidence shows that warmth judgments are primary. That is, warmth is judged before competence, and warmth carries greater weight in affecting social reactions.[11-13]

> *"While both warmth and competence consistently rise to the top of attributes in all studies, evidence shows that warmth judgments are primary."*

We've already established that people infer warmth from the perceived motives and intentions of another person,[14] and that those perceptions are gleaned not only from voluntary actions but also from involuntary messages the other person conveys.

So, in order for our intentions to be perceived as warmth, it's vital that we emanate the related traits that science has identified from the warmth attribute. These include:

- pure intent

- friendliness

- helpfulness

- sincerity

- trustworthiness

- and morality (doing the right thing)

These are the signals we want our autonomic system to be sending.

Take a moment and contrast this list with the primary drivers/motivators that you listed in the exercise at the beginning of the chapter. Is there a difference?

Most people who complete the exercise reveal motivators and drivers similar to, "I want to get paid," or "I want something money can buy." When your prospect senses that your intention is "all about you" they become more guarded.

As a sales manager I've received both good and bad feedback regarding salespeople. One client said they could tell the salesperson was only in it for himself, and they refused to do business with him. To describe their interaction with this salesperson, the client coined a term that has stuck in my mind forever; he called it "commission breath." It fits so perfectly. That is exactly the type of feeling we are trying to avoid.

Prospective buyers experience a great deal of concern and trepidation (especially when the product is beyond their own area of expertise). Their ignorance creates risk for them. They are concerned that an unscrupulous salesperson could take advantage of them—that they'll be sold the wrong product or at the very least they won't get the best value. And when a client decides that a salesperson's intentions are not aligned with their best interests, in most cases, the deal is off.

Often, even when our intentions are good, the larger the opportunity is, the harder it is not to think about what's in it for us. It is ironic then, that despite our intent to earn money in an ethical way, when we enter an interaction with our minds focused on what *we* get out of the interaction, our autonomic system sends precisely the wrong signal for the best outcome.

"When we focus on what we get out of an interaction our autonomic system sends precisely the wrong signal for the best outcome."

Recall the two subconscious determinations that take place in the first seconds of any interaction:

1. What is this person's intent (good or bad)?

2. Does this person have the ability to execute that intention?

These are the two determinations that buyers are making each time they meet with us.

When it comes to purchasing something outside our experience, because of our ignorance, there is no question that the sales agent has the upper hand and the *ability* to possibly take advantage of us. Our inexperience leaves us vulnerable, and therefore, we must rely primarily on the first measurable discriminator—intent.

It is precisely because intent is so heavily weighted in sales situations that we must transmit the right intentions. The key is to adopt a mindset that will have us transmitting the right intentions—one where we genuinely want to help the other person in a friendly and ethical way. There is no need to change your personality or become something you are not.

By genuinely trying to help the other person in a friendly and ethical way our autonomic system will take over and automatically transmit all the right messages. I often marvel at the sublime beauty in this altruistic dynamic.

How to Adopt the Right Mindset

I can hear you now, "For heaven's sake, James! I bought a book about closing. Why are you going on and on about mindset and good intentions?"

I'll tell you why. Because intent matters more than technique.[15]

Let that sink in for a moment.

I can teach you effective techniques, but if you enter the opportunity with "commission breath" it won't matter. Conversely, when a client can detect your genuine intention to help, you can butcher the technique, say gobbledygook and it will still work out. Intent matters more than technique.

So the question now becomes, "How do I get myself into the right mindset?"

As it turns out, we can look to science for help here, as well. There are three simple steps you can take before any interaction to adopt the right mindset:

1. Lose the ego.

2. Create positive emotion.

3. Enter with the right intent.

1. Lose the Ego

Ego is about you and self-importance—either what you hope to receive or the desire to impress others. A strong sense of self-esteem is good and important to the concept of competency. At the same time, because warmth and intention are weighted more heavily in sales situations, our primary concern is to maximize our warmth factor and transmit that we have the client's best interests at heart.

Enter your initial interactions without any ego-based agenda. Lose the ego. Remain confident and competent, but enter the initial interaction *tabula rasa* (with a blank slate) and no defined agenda other than how you can best help the prospective client.

Having an objective is indeed important and later we will discuss setting up primary and secondary objectives. However, in your initial meetings your goal is to project maximum warmth, genuineness, friendliness, helpfulness, and good intention.

Ego-driven desires cause your autonomic system to send the wrong signals. By losing your ego you will be in the right mindset, and your body will transmit the right messages.

2. Create Positive Emotion

Consider using these recall and a posture techniques to create the ideal emotional state before your meetings.

Positive Recall

The positive recall technique is simple. Recall a time when you really felt friendly and helpful. Remember, what science tells us we're going for here is pure intent, friendliness, helpfulness, sincerity, trustworthiness, and morality. What did it look, sound, smell, feel, and taste like? Make it as vivid as possible, and try to relive the experience.

Here is as an example of a memory I use before meeting with new prospects:

One day, out of the blue, I received a call from a long-time friend. He shared that his company had a new product they were trying to market. My friend was not in sales, and he asked me to visit their office and coach them on how they might improve sales. He wasn't hiring me as a consultant; he was simply asking for a favor. I could tell he was calling because they were in trouble. Naturally, I agreed to help.

Despite this being described as a "casual chat" with his company's top executives, I understood that by bringing me in, he was putting his reputation on the line. So it was important to me that this meeting reflect well on my friend. I invested some time learning all about their product, their processes, the new market they were in, and their results thus far. Out of respect for my friend I wanted the meeting to be as helpful as possible.

At the beginning of the meeting I described what I believed I had uncovered about their situation and asked if I was on target. I wasn't. About 20% of the information I had gathered was incorrect. After these top executives corrected the information and filled in the gaps, we entered into a productive conversation about what I had seen work elsewhere and different ways we could approach their situation.

It was an ultra-productive session where I was freely sharing my experience, and they were receiving new and helpful information. They were so engaged that they bumped their next meeting to continue the conversation. We concluded with an excellent vibe, and they thanked me profusely. As their CEO walked me to the parking lot he asked what he owed me for the visit. I explained that I was doing it out of friendship for my buddy.

Weeks later, my friend shared that they had experienced great success with some of the ideas we discussed. Then unexpectedly I received a check in the mail from the CEO along with a thank-you note. It was quite a surprise. I recall feeling satisfied and validated that I had truly been helpful that day.

This is just one of the memories I use before meeting with prospective clients to get me into a helpful mindset. Once you're able to re-experience the emotion of your memory, your autonomic system will take care of the rest. Ideally, spend about two minutes doing this to let the physiological processes take effect, and your body will begin telegraphing that you are genuinely trying to help in a friendly and ethical way.[16]

Posture to Improve Emotion and Physiology

The posture technique comes from the relatively new discoveries made by Amy Cuddy and Dana Carney who discovered that postural expressions not only affect people's emotions, but amazingly, they also affect hormone levels.[17-19] Cuddy and Carney discovered that by *faking* body postures associated with the desired emotion, people can positively improve their hormone response. Assuming *power poses,* for example, increases people's testosterone, decreases their cortisol, increases their appetite for risk, and causes them to perform better in job interviews.[20]

For our purpose we want to adopt a posture of friendliness, helpfulness, sincerity, and trustworthiness. To invoke the emotion (and ideal hormonal and physiology), here is the posture we want to adopt:

Arms are open, rounded and relaxed about waist height. Palms are tilted about 45 degrees upwards. Shoulders are relaxed and down (not up near the neck). Legs are not crossed and may even be stretched apart a bit past shoulder width, if it is comfortable. Smile warmly.

"Mock Hug" Welcoming Gesture

Consider the whole posture as a *mock hug* or welcoming gesture. Casually and with flowing variation, maintain this posture for two minutes or so. According to research, it takes two minutes for the hormone response to kick in.[21]

As a reminder, both of these exercises are to be done before your meeting. With a little bit of practice you'll find that you can do them both simultaneously.

3. Enter with the Right Intent

Positive self-talk improves performance in decision making, strategy formulation, academics, sports, overcoming dysfunctions and bad habits, and other complex skills.[22-27]

To program our autonomic system to transmit the right intent, we are simply going to use a couple of affirmations by asking ourselves a question or two that will quickly prime our body to send the right messages about our intent.

Being genuine, say and ask yourself these things before your interaction:

- "You know, I genuinely care about this client. I'm excited to see what they have going on."

- "I'm sure I can help these guys. I can't wait to see what I can do for this client."

- "I want to make a big difference for these guys."

- "I'm curious to learn how I can best help these people. I'm thrilled to find out what I can do for them."

These statements (when said genuinely) will cause you to project the right intentions to others.

Remember, that between the balance of warmth and competence, warmth is weighted more heavily than competence because the prospective client is outside of their area of experience. So projecting the right intention is critical.

It's easy to see how this works, so consider creating some of your own affirmations and questions that tie closely to your line of work. Just remember to tie them back to the traits that science has determined are the most important:

- pure intent

- friendliness

- helpfulness

- sincerity

- trustworthiness

- and morality (doing the right thing)

Share Your Intent

All of the exercises to this point are intended to be done before meeting with your client and can be completed in less than three to five minutes. This prepares you and your autonomic system to transmit the right signals in the first seconds of your interaction, which is important because that's when judgments regarding your warmth and intention happen.

However, there is something you can do while in the presence of your client to project the right intention—actually say it. Tell the client what your intentions are. They will still look for congruence between your verbalization and your body language, and when they match, you will improve your impression by yet another level.

There are many ways to share your intent with clients, and you will need to adjust your message depending on the context of the meeting. So with that in mind, here are some examples to help you create your own intention statements.

Sometimes, short and sweet works. Early in my career I had a technical resource role and was always paired up with another salesperson. So after introducing myself, I'd simply add, "My job is to make sure you get what you want." That always resonated with clients and accurately conveyed that I was their advocate.

Very often prospects will jump the gun and ask for pricing or competitive differentiators before any of the preliminaries are complete. Sometimes I get a question like, "Why should we purchase you over your competition?" When that question is premature I'll often respond with something along the lines of, "Well I think we might be a good match, but I'm not 100% confident yet. My goal is to get you a solution that exactly matches what you want. Share with me a little about…" In this way I convey that I suspect potential exists, but as their advocate I would like to know more about them and what they are trying to accomplish.

With the early pricing question I often use something along these lines, "My whole career, my formula for success has simply been to do a great job for clients, and then those clients in return have helped me get new business. That means it's not important that I get maximum profit from a deal. I just need to make sure I am in the black. So I promise I'll get you the best deal possible once we know there is a great fit." Sometimes I'll then redirect to discovery with, "So with that in mind can you share with me…?"

Now this dialogue accomplishes many things, but what I want to accentuate here is that my intent to get them the best deal possible is conveyed, and that lets us move on to the important details without getting embroiled into a conversation about price.

Another way you can convey your intent is to weave it into your introduction about your company and culture. An example might be, "What I've come to learn after X years in the business is that every client is unique. So our goal is to get you a solution that is exactly what you want.

Most of the time we can do that—but not always—and by working togeth-er, we can identify all the dimensions of what you're looking for, and make sure we have a solution that exactly meets your needs." In this way we are conveying our intention that we want what they want, and that will allow us to smoothly move through the process of understanding each other.

These examples should get your juices flowing so you can create your own intention statements that will be congruent with the messages your autonomic system is sending. Together they strongly communicate your intentions to genuinely help the other person in a friendly and ethical way.

Closing Secret #5 - Intent matters more than technique.

Conclusion

Having the right mindset will improve your experience, your prospective client's experience, and improve your outcomes in a most positive way. The techniques described in this chapter will get your mindset in the right place and get your autonomic systems transmitting the right messages, in as little as three to five minutes.

After you have practiced it consistently for some time, you will discover that you are simply always in the mindset. It will become a permanent part of you, and you will automatically transmit this signal 24/7. This is an amazing state to be in from a happiness and personal achievement per-spective and may be worth as much as the rest of the techniques you are about to learn. It also hints at a deeper meaning of what selling is—service with pure intent. I encourage you to adopt it not just in selling but also in your everyday life.

To discover more about the latest science and research in this fascinating area, visit PureMuir.com where you can find additional commentary and resources. In the next chapter we will learn about one of the biggest fac-tors in sales success.

CHAPTER 4

Planning = Success

"There is one common ingredient that links virtually
all successful people to their success:
Well-planned goals."

–Jeb Blount

Sales planning is strongly correlated with sales success.[1, 2] For example, an international study of business-to-business sales teams found that the most effective sales groups (effectiveness being measured in terms of sales volume, market share, profitability, and customer satisfaction) were better at sales planning in all areas including: planning each sales call, planning sales strategies for each customer, planning coverage of assigned territory and customer responsibility, and planning daily activities.[3]

Neil Rackham says it this way, "A consistent finding about successful salespeople is that they put effort into planning. Good selling depends on good planning more than any other single factor."[4]

"A consistent finding about successful salespeople is that they put effort into planning. Good selling depends on good planning more than any other single factor." –Neil Rackham

---

Unfortunately, research also shows that despite the correlation between planning and sales success, most sales people do not set realistic goals for themselves for each sales encounter.[4]

Our objective in the next few chapters is to make you an excellent planner by:

- Describing what Sales Objectives and Call Objectives are

- Defining what makes a good Sales Objective and Call Objective

- How to set Call Objectives for each sales opportunity

- And most importantly, how to set up individual Call Objectives for each sales encounter

By doing these things consistently and in the right way, we will be staging each of your opportunities in such a way that each of your outcomes will always be improved.

Why Are You Engaging Your Client?

Before we get started try this quick exercise: Take five opportunities that you are currently working, and quickly answer this question for each one, "Why are you engaging this prospect at this time?"

Save your answers. We will return to them in a moment.

Do You Have Clarity?

The underlying principle behind all planning and goal setting is clarity. By being clear about what we really want from each opportunity and on each individual sales encounter, we set forces in motion (both conscious and unconscious) that move us towards the achievement of our goals.

It is important then, that we seek clarity about what is wanted in each opportunity and each sales encounter. I distinguish between opportunities and sales encounters because when asked what their goal is for a given sales encounter, the vast majority of salespeople reply with something equivalent to "close the sale" or "get the order."

Unfortunately, in all but the simplest transactions the typical sales cycle may involve from four to ten sales encounters. For very complex sales it can be even more. So the idea that you are going to close the sale (as lofty as that goal may be) on any of the earliest encounters is completely unrealistic. Closing the sale is really only a realistic accomplishment on the last call of the cycle.

> *"Closing the sale is really only a realistic accomplishment on the last call of the cycle."*

It is important then that we distinguish between our overall sales objective and our individual call objectives on any given opportunity. Doing so gives us both the big picture of what we want to accomplish with our sale (the overall sales objective) and what we wish to accomplish on this particular call (the call objective).

As we will see, setting appropriate sales objectives for each opportunity and appropriate call objectives for each individual encounter will lead to an unbroken chain of successful advances that will ultimately lead to closing the sale and getting the order.

What's the Difference Between Sales Objectives & Call Objectives?

Sales objectives and call objectives have very specific criteria and knowing their criteria will make your use of The Perfect Close much more successful. So for clarity let us define here both sales objectives and call objectives.

Sales Objective - the revenue (or outcome) you anticipate generating by closing this particular *opportunity* with this particular client.

Call Objective - an advance or commitment that is the desired outcome of this particular sales *encounter* with this particular person or group.

The contrast here is that the sales objective is your ultimate goal of closing this *specific opportunity* while call objectives are our goals for achieving an advance on each particular *sales call or encounter*.

The clearer these two are for you the more rapidly you will reach your desired outcome. As an aid to you we have developed a specific set of criteria for each that will help you make your sales objectives and each call objective crystal clear. If you are experienced and already familiar with these concepts feel free to skip to the next chapter.

How to Set Sales Objectives

Consider one of the sales opportunities you are working. What is the outcome that you want to achieve at the conclusion of your efforts? The clearer you are, the easier it is to leverage the activities that help you achieve that aim.

It is common for people to be confused about their ultimate goal and the goal of their most immediate next step. By stripping away the clutter that may exist between the two, we can achieve clarity that gives us perspective as well as the impulse to take the next best action.

In general, your overall sales objective defines the reason you are meeting with this particular prospect. The achievement of this objective could be six months away or as soon as the next encounter. If you don't have an overall sales objective when meeting with a client then you are, quite literally, meeting for nothing. There is no good reason for you to be there.

Remember, time is a valuable and limited resource for everyone. It's the ultimate equalizer. So invest it wisely and always respect the time of others. Don't waste time. There should be value for our clients every time we meet with them.

Your overall sales objective answers the question, "What do I want to happen with this client that isn't happening now?" Your answer to that question should be specific and measurable.

A well-defined sales objective includes the following:

1. It is related to a specific product or service.

2. It is specific and measurable.

3. It has a specific target date for completion.

4. It should be realistic from the client's perspective.

Related to a specific product or service - Because it is a *sales* objective, it should be related to the specific product or service that you intend to sell to this particular client at this particular time. If you offer more than one product or service, then your objective should clearly state exactly which products and services are part of this particular objective. Related products and services can be bundled together into a single objective (i.e. a package). However if you are engaged in offering more than one unrelated product or service to this prospective client, then you should have a separate sales objective for each specific product or service.

Specific and measurable - Your sales objective should quantify the specific *quantity* of products or services that you are intending to sell. For example, if it is licenses then it will be the number of licenses you intend to sell; if it is service hours then it will be the number of hours; if it is for a term of service then it will be for a length of time (e.g. 36 months); and so on. When your objective is achieved it should be easy to measure its accomplishment. You should know, 1. If it was achieved or not, and 2. How close your objective was compared to what was actually sold.

Have a target date for completion - This is the likely timeframe for the completion of this specific sales objective. When do you expect that this sales objective will be accomplished? This timeframe should be realistic from the client's perspective.

Realistic from the client's perspective - All three of the previous criteria should be realistic from the client's perspective—not just yours. No wishful thinking here. No including products they are unlikely to buy. No astronomical quantities. No timeframes that would be impossible for the client to pull off. These criteria should be realistic from the client's perspective based on what is happening for that client right now. Sometimes we do sell more than we expected and even sooner than we anticipated, but we want our sales objective to reflect what is realistic right now, and we can still hope and plan for the best.

So for each sales objective you should be able to answer the following:

- The client I am engaging is...

- The product/service I am trying to sell is...

- The amount of the product/service I am trying to sell is...

- The date for this to be completed is...

Rephrased into a single sentence, it might look like this:

"I am engaging [client] with the intent to sell [amount] of [product/service] by [date]."

The main benefit to creating a sales objective for each opportunity is clarity. There is another major benefit, however. By creating sales objectives that meet all of the important criteria (specific product, measurable, target date, and realistic) you will find that your sales forecast is much more accurate.

I want to sidebar here and state that in order to create a realistic sales objective you should have discovered some things about your prospective client (how to perform a productive discovery will be a topic of a future work). If you haven't had the opportunity to do discovery or haven't had much of a conversation with your prospective client yet, then:

1. Do what research you can prior to your next contact, and

2. Make discovery the objective of your next meeting.

You cannot ascertain what the solution (product, quantity, timeframe) would look like or whether it is realistic without a discussion with your prospective client. Prescription without diagnosis is malpractice. Once you have met with the client and determined the scope of their need, you can craft your sales objective.

"Prescription without diagnosis is malpractice."

In some sales it is possible to have a reasonable idea of what the scope of the opportunity will be before you have met with the client. In this case you may have developed a value hypothesis and estimated a solution prior to having met. In fact you may have used this value hypothesis as a means to engage the prospective client. If that is the case, just remember that these estimates are just that—estimates. Only after you have met with the client and determined the actual scope of their need is it appropriate to craft your sales objective.

What Are Your Opportunities Telling You?

Now pull out your list of five opportunities from our quick exercise at the beginning of the chapter. Review them, and answer the following questions.

- Do they each contain the four elements of a sales objective?

- How closely do they compare?

- Is there a pattern to any element that might have been missing?

- What needs to be added to make each one a complete sales objective?

For many people, this is an eye-opening exercise the first time they perform it. What most professionals discover is that on average, they have only one or two of the four elements of a well-defined sales objective. And because the sales objective is the foundation for the *call objective* (which is even more important), having a well-defined sales objective for each of your opportunities will make each of your individual sales encounters more effective.

Take the time to craft a well-defined sales objective for every opportunity that you are actively working.

Closing Secret #6 - Planning = Success

Conclusion

The Sales Objective is the foundation of the Call Objective. Having an effective call objective is a key element to maximizing The Perfect Close. Having clarity in each of your sales opportunities will make each of your individual sales encounters more effective. In the next chapter we will explore the differences between advances, closes, and a new concept called *continuations*—and why knowing the difference can make a big difference in your selling efforts.

James Muir

CHAPTER 5

The Critical Advance

"Without a 'next step' you are likely working with someone who is fully not engaged. A 'next step' is a crucial delineator between real opportunities and pretend opportunities."

–Tibor Shanto

Why Bother with the Distinction Between an *Advance* and a *Close*?

E arlier in this work we touched on the concept of closing and advancing the sale. After this chapter we will use these terms synonymously for the most part. To the concepts of *closing* and *advancing* we now add the concept of a *continuation* also introduced by Neil Rackham.

It is very important to understand the difference between these three concepts because not knowing can cause your sales to drag on and on in a never-ending state of non-closure.

Here are the definitions of each:

Close - a firm commitment to buy. It is the consummation of the sale and the final order that marks the transition from evaluating to actual ownership and use of the product or solution.

Advance - a significant action that requires energy by the client—either in the call or right after it—that moves the sale toward a decision.

Continuation - a situation where the sale will continue yet no specific action has been agreed upon by the customer to move forward.

There is an obvious demarcation when a *close* takes place, so it's pretty clear when an opportunity becomes closed. It is worth mentioning, however, that even when we have a firm verbal commitment to buy, if paperwork or contracts are needed to complete the sale, the sale is not completed until the contracts are authorized by the client.

It's between the advance and the continuation that confusion can set in. Without a clear understanding of the difference between these two you will be doomed to potentially endless, time-consuming churn and needlessly long decision cycles. You will also be unsure about where you really stand in any given opportunity, which in turn, will cause forecasting issues.

As a VP of Sales I've had the opportunity to work with a tremendous number of salespeople and their many different opportunities. I've found it's quite common for professionals (even those dedicated to 100% selling) to misunderstand the differences between a sales advance and a continuation. One rep I managed demonstrates this perfectly. Let me illustrate:

> *"It's quite common for professionals (even those dedicated to 100% selling) to misunderstand the differences between a sales advance and a continuation."*

When I accepted a regional VP role, I met with each of my team members to review the opportunities they were working. One rep was absolutely convinced that he had a great opportunity on the line. The problem was, what should have been a relatively short sales cycle had gone on for almost a year. After reviewing this and other opportunities with him we began to dig into what was happening on each contact and visit with the prospective client. A pattern emerged. I would ask the rep to describe the events during a particular visit and its outcome, and here are just a few of his replies:

- From an early contact, "They mentioned they know client XYZ and really respect them. I sent them literature."

- At an on-site visit, "I gathered a lot of great information."

- During an early encounter, "It was great. I did a demonstration, and they said they were really impressed."

- On another visit, "We did lunch, and I suggested she look at one of our whitepapers which I provided."

- On a phone call, "They asked me to come to the office next time I was in the area."

- Upon visiting, "They acknowledged that we have some really great stuff, and I offered them a sample project plan."

- Yet another contact, "We did a second demo over the web."

- A visit, "We did lunch and really strengthened our relationship."

- Later, "She thought it might make sense to see another demo."

- Another visit, "I visited and collected some really useful information."

- And yet another call, "I asked them if they wanted a proposal and cost estimate, and they agreed."

On and on it went like this for nearly twelve months.

What's going on here? Are these not signs that we have an engaged prospective client? Barely. Here's why: Go back and review each response, but this time ask yourself, "What action did the *client* take during or after each contact?"

Was the client investing any real energy in moving the project forward? No. Beyond time spent at lunch and some visits, this client was not investing any real energy in moving forward.

Here is where my rep went wrong—none of these are *advances*. They are all *continuations*.

An *advance* is a **significant action that requires energy by the client**—either during the call or right after it—that moves the sale toward a decision.

A *continuation* is a situation where the sale will continue yet **no specific action has been agreed upon by the customer** to move forward.

My rep had completed a tremendous number of tasks while the client had performed none. And unfortunately, this rep's entire pipeline was filled with opportunities just like this one—all continuing endlessly; all going nowhere. Needless to say it was affecting the rep's income in a negative way.

For me, it is something of a hobby to understand what makes each sales rep tick and to identify their individual patterns that contribute to their success or failures, so I continued probing the mindset of this rep by asking, "How do you know if a sales call has been successful? What tells you?"

His reply was something that is very common among less experienced professionals. He said, "If they show interest, or if I improve the relationship or collect useful information."

"Hmm…, how can you tell if a client is interested?" I asked.

He explained, "If they say they are interested or clearly show they are interested with their expression and body language."

I'll bet most people would actually agree with this statement, but it's not good enough. If we use loose criteria like this then your sales calls will be doomed to potentially endless continuations and unnecessarily long sales cycles.

I asked, "What is your goal going into each sales situation?"

He replied, "I only ask for a contract when they are ready, so my goal is usually to share some information with them, strengthen the relationship, or gather useful information."

Again, I would wager that most people would agree that these are positive activities in the context of the sales cycle. Here's the problem—it's just not good enough.

What Is the Value of Your Time?

As professionals in any field (sales or otherwise) the only true asset we have is our time. How we invest our time determines our happiness and success in relationships, business, and everything we do.

The value we produce comes from the investment of our time. It is *all* we have. Therefore, it is critical that we invest it in the best ways possible.

> *"As professionals in any field (sales or otherwise) the only true asset we have is our time. How we invest our time determines our happiness and success in relationships, business, and everything we do."*

Because my rep did not understand the difference between an advance and a continuation he was wasting a tremendous amount of time. Even worse, that lack of understanding was causing him to do things that were actually *lengthening* his sales cycles. He was the source of his own problems.

Ultimately, once he learned what you are about to learn regarding the differences between advances and continuations, he went on to be extremely successful.

Are You Efficient or Effective?

It is natural when attempting to improve our productivity that we immediately seek to do the things we already know, just faster. This is because we are drawing upon information within us—the processes we already know—as the basis for our improvement. We seek to do the things we know, just more efficiently.

My rep in the story above was already very efficient by any standard and pouring a ton of energy into his opportunities. Unfortunately, his energy was focused on doing the wrong things (and only very slightly so). Yet this slight difference was causing him to underachieve his potential in a very big way.

This then, is the difference between efficiency and effectiveness.

Efficiency is reducing the time it takes to do something.

Effectiveness is doing the right things.

Improving effectiveness requires assessing all of the things we can do to produce results and adopting those things that produce the best outcomes. The challenge is, we don't know what we don't know. That is, we are not always aware of all the possible alternatives to the methods we are currently using. For this reason, improving effectiveness often requires help from someone with a perspective different than our own.

My rep was inadvertently seeking engagements that would result in continuations. Once he understood this and learned how to instead create advances, his results improved dramatically.

Remember:

An *advance* is a **significant action that requires energy by the client**, either during the call or right after it that moves the sale toward a decision.

A *continuation* is a situation where the sale will continue yet **no specific action has been agreed upon by the customer** to move forward.

The two critical elements in these definitions are action and energy.

Observing the action and energy a prospective client expends during or immediately following a meeting accomplishes two very important things:

1. It tells us just how engaged the prospect is, and

2. It (potentially) moves the sales process one step closer to closure.

In general, the larger the sacrifice the client is willing to make to continue the process (i.e. energy expended), the better the indicator that they are serious about moving forward, and therefore worth our investment of time. It is a litmus test of sorts that we can use to qualify our prospective clients.

"The larger the sacrifice the client is willing to make to continue the process, the better the indicator that they are serious about moving forward, and therefore worth our investment of time."

My rep in the story was never doing this. He was never really challenging his clients in a way that would test their commitment to change. On the contrary, he was actually volunteering to do work for them with little or no reciprocity on their side.

For example, if assessment work needed to be done on their side before the process could continue, he would often volunteer to complete it for them. Now, this service is not inherently bad, however, it reduces the salesperson's role from that of a professional collaborating to find a solution to that of a service representative. What does it tell us about the urgency a client feels when they are not willing to invest energy into the process?

In contrast, what if his client had already independently completed an exhaustive assessment that went above and beyond what was needed and documented it in a 30 page report? What would that tell us about their level of commitment?

This is what my rep was missing. By doing *for* the client, he learned nothing about the client's sense of urgency, nor their level of commitment toward finding a solution. By offering to do everything and never committing prospective clients to do anything he was missing out on an opportunity to gauge their commitment to the project. This was causing him to spend time on unqualified prospects. It was also virtually impossible for him to accurately forecast the likelihood of any opportunity coming to fruition.

Let me sidebar here and say that there is nothing inherently wrong with offering to render free services to prospective clients to further a sales opportunity. However, this should be done with great caution because no client will turn down the value of a free service if it requires no commitment on their own behalf. Without a clear understanding of when such a thing is actually advancing a sale you may fall into the same trap my rep did and invest a great deal of time in opportunities that will never pay off.

How did we solve the problem? All it took was teaching my rep the difference between an advance and a continuation and getting him to make the objective of each call an advance. Once he accomplished this, the issue went away, and he more than doubled his sales from the previous year.

What Is the Acid Test for Advances?

The acid test for an advance is action and energy. By setting call objectives that require action and energy on behalf of your prospective client you will have a clear understanding of their commitment level while continually moving your sale toward closure.

If the client is not taking an action, it is not an advance.

If the action the client takes requires little to no energy, it is not an advance.

Examples of advances might include:

- Arrange for you to meet with a higher-level decision maker

- Agree to meet with your technical team and invest time to discuss requirements and options

- Share sensitive information needed for an assessment

- Arranging a group meeting with executives for you to review the details of your proposed solution face-to-face

- Have a meeting or conversation with a reference you provide

All of these require both action and a decent amount of energy (or perhaps even personal risk in the case of the introduction).

As it turns out, there is a wide spectrum of possible advances in any given sale that range from very little commitment of time and energy to those requiring a great deal of commitment.

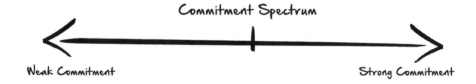

The key, then, is in the setting of our call objectives.

"The acid test for an advance is action and energy."

Recall what my rep answered when questioned about his goal for a typical call, "I only ask for a contract when they are ready, so my goal is usually to share some information with them, strengthen the relationship, or gather useful information."

Unfortunately, "sharing information," "strengthening the relationship," and "gathering information" are all continuations. None of these require much action or energy on behalf of the client. And to be frank, every call provides the opportunity to share and gather information and should always improve the relationship. The problem with these types of objectives is that they lead to continuations not advances.

So the solution for my rep was simply to set up true advances as primary and secondary objectives on each call. Before we discuss exactly how to do that, let us first discuss some of the psychology and science behind sales advances, and why they improve your sales outcomes.

The Science Behind Advancing the Sale

Two scientific concepts reveal why the practice of setting sales advances is so effective:

1. Commitment/Consistency

2. Endowed Progress

Commitment/Consistency: Once we have committed to an idea or goal, either verbally or in writing, we are strongly compelled to honor that commitment in order to remain congruent with our self image. We convince ourselves that we have done the right thing and feel better about our decision by remaining consistent.[1]

More importantly, once we accept small commitments we become more willing to commit ourselves even further along those same lines—our actions become increasingly consistent toward achieving the end goal.[2] Persuasion psychology expert Robert Cialdini has devoted an entire chapter to this topic in his excellent book *Influence: Science and Practice.*

This psychology is the first key to understanding why using advances to further our sales is so effective. Once a prospective client has agreed to take a step forward, there is a strong compulsion to remain consistent with the process and take an additional step, and another, and another. In this way each advance further increases the likelihood that our prospective client will take another step in a chain of advances that lead to the ultimate conclusion of the sale.

Interestingly, the closer a prospect is to the end of the process the more committed they become to it. That is the essence of our second concept.

Endowed Progress: Once we feel that we have made progress toward a goal we become even more committed toward continued effort in achieving that goal. In fact, the closer we get to the goal, the more our effort increases.[3]

You can think of this concept simply as *closure*. Once we set out to attain something (say the acquisition of a new solution or service, for example) the closer we get to completion, the more our efforts to do so accelerate.

Many things can be done to increase the client's perception of just how far along they are. And interestingly, studies indicate that the *perception* of progress is as effective as actual progress in getting clients to accelerate their efforts. That is the *endowed* part of Endowed Progress.

So, making a client aware that they are closer toward their goal than they may have realized and communicating to them how much progress they are making toward their goal will accelerate their efforts toward closure.

These two dynamics, *commitment/consistency* and *endowed progress*, are the two primary psychological reasons why utilizing sales advances is so effective in improving sales outcomes. Once the initial small advance (the commitment part) is achieved, clients are likely to take another second small step and so forth. Additionally, the more progress the client makes toward closure (the endowed progress part), the more accelerated their efforts become.

"These two things: commitment/consistency and endowed progress are the two primary psychological reasons why utilizing sales advances is so effective in improving sales outcomes."

Done correctly, these two principles of advancing the sale (commitment/consistency and endowed progress) represent a virtuous cycle in which each component synergistically aids the other in ultimately closing the sale.

They key lies in the setting of our *call objectives* which is the subject of our next chapter.

<u>*Closing Secret #7*</u> - Knowing the difference between an advance and a continuation can mean the difference between success and failure.

Conclusion

Understanding the distinctions between a continuation and an advance and why advances improve sales outcomes is integral to setting effective objectives for each sales interaction. Setting advances (rather than continuations) is key to making The Perfect Close work. Become proficient at setting advances as your primary and secondary objectives for each sales encounter, and you will dramatically increase your sales outcomes.

How to effectively set call objectives is the subject of our next chapter.

James Muir

CHAPTER 6

How to Set Call Objectives

"The true goal for a salesperson is to help the customer win."

–Mike Weinberg

The way to achieve your ultimate Sales Objective is through the completion of incremental Call Objectives (Advances). By setting appropriate call objectives for each visit and encounter we will achieve an unbroken chain of successful advances that will ultimately lead to *closing the sale* and *getting the order.*

"By setting appropriate call objectives for each visit and encounter we will achieve an unbroken chain of successful advances that will ultimately lead to closing the sale and getting the order."

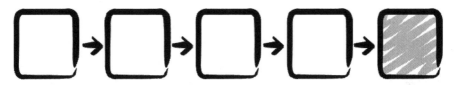

Incremental Advances are key to closing the sale.

Take a minute and consider a recent appointment that took place in each of the five sales opportunities you selected in the previous chapter.

Briefly write down what you were hoping to achieve on each call.

We will come back to these in a moment.

I find that people often have difficulty articulating exactly what they were hoping to accomplish in sales calls and meetings. It's almost like they are thinking, "I'll engage them and just see what happens." This is just hoping that something will happen, and as the late Rick Page used to say, "Hope is not a strategy."

There are some common mistakes made when setting call objectives, and it is easy to fall into these pitfalls. The three most common are:

1. The call objective is too general and not specific.

2. The call objective is unrealistic.

3. The call objective is not really an advance.

Let's explore these in a little more depth.

The Call Objective is too general - Call objectives should be specific and measurable. When the call objective is vague or general, it is all too easy to depart the encounter not really knowing whether or not it was achieved. Vague call objectives such as *keep the momentum going* will leave you completely unclear about the direction you've gone and the progress you've made when the encounter is finished. Each call objective should be specific enough that it is a simple matter to know at the end of the call whether or not it was accomplished.

The Call Objective is unrealistic - Initially when asked, most professionals will state that the objective of their call is to "close the deal." But as we have noted previously, in all but the simplest transactions, actually closing the business is only realistic on the *last* step of the sale. It is also possible to set call objectives that are farther along the sales cycle than the prospect is ready for at the moment. For example, it is unlikely that your call will result in scheduling a site visit to a plant located on another continent before you have discussed your initial value proposition. We will discuss setting up your call objectives in a moment. The takeaway here is that your call objective be realistic from the client's perspective.

The Call Objective is not really an advance - Remember, an advance is a significant action that *requires energy by the client*, either during or immediately following the call that moves the sale toward a decision. That means that call objectives like, "demonstrate the ABC module," or "persuade Dave of so and so..." are not advances, because they are not client-driven. Rather, the salesperson is thinking of what they (the salesperson) will do rather than what the client will do.

Setting a call objective that is not an advance is a very common pitfall. Remember that the acid test for an advance is action and energy. By setting call objectives that require both action and energy *on behalf of our prospective client* we will get a clear understanding of their commitment level while continually moving the sale toward closure.

If the client is not taking an action, it is not an advance.

If the action the client takes requires little to no energy, it is not an advance.

Pull out that list you just made regarding what you were hoping to accomplish on those recent appointments. Note whether or not you accomplished your goal for that appointment, and then answer the following questions:

1. Were they specific and measurable? Could you easily tell if they were accomplished or not?

2. Were they realistic from the client's perspective?

3. Were they true advances?

   a. Were they client-focused? (things the client would do)

   b. Did they require action and energy on the client's behalf?

   c. Were they something that would move the sale forward?

4. Is there any pattern to the type of call objectives you have been setting in the past?

Until professionals receive training it is extremely common for their call objectives to focus on what they, the professional, will do rather than being client-focused and centered on what we want the client to do.

Ignoring the client, their buying cycle, and considering only your own activities and sales cycle is one of the biggest mistakes in professional selling. Here is the challenge it creates in relation to call planning:

> *"Ignoring the client, their buying cycle, and considering only your own activities and sales cycle is one of the biggest mistakes in professional selling."*

When you complete your planned action (giving a presentation, let's say) you tend to feel good about yourself, and your prospective client may even reflect this good feeling. This can blind you to assessing their true commitment level, since *good feelings* are not the acid test for an advance—only action and energy are. And because no action or commitment on behalf of the client has been given, we may leave the encounter thinking there is solid interest, when in fact, we have no real evidence of that.

Multi-million Dollar Indulgence

Let me illustrate. One of our reps had an opportunity where the estimated initial investment was north of $1 Million, and because the organization had many child companies, there would be many additional sales to follow.

Our rep's primary contact was a new CIO at one of the child companies who had recently been hired from one of our existing accounts. Knowing of the change and the CIO's support for our solution, our rep convinced him to let us do a demonstration and orientation as the first step.

The initial meeting included the new CIO and two of his staff. Because the CIO was already familiar with the solution, the meeting came off with no surprises. Our rep then engaged the new CIO to show others within the larger organization, and the new CIO agreed to set it up.

The organization was quite large and this turned into many separate demonstrations which took place over several months. It was reported that many of the demonstrations were spectacular and met with great response. Repeatedly, our rep was able to leverage one demonstration in order to get another. All of these meetings were going well, so the rep began to forecast a positive outcome for the sale.

Once a prospective deal of significant size hits a high probability in the sales forecast, it garners attention from executive management. So as you can imagine, this particular opportunity was beginning to be looked upon with interest by our organization's upper management.

Around this time the rep asked the CIO if he would be interested in seeing a proposal, and the new CIO agreed. Our rep felt this was a big step forward in the sale. In the meantime, my rep continued the demo parade throughout the organization.

As our rep and the CIO discussed the proposal, the new CIO mentioned that his organization had a very onerous legal process. In response, our rep suggested we get them a copy of our standard agreement to which he agreed. This activity was translated by our rep as "they requested a copy of the contract." Our executive management team deemed this a very strong sign of progress and that's when I was asked to get involved and meet with the newly hired CIO.

What I discovered, unfortunately, was that the new CIO had very little influence on the rest of the organization, and that he had agreed to everything—the demos, the proposal, and the sample agreement—because he was friends with our rep. He genuinely hoped that all the demos and meetings would create a grass-roots demand for a system change, but in reality the executive management in his organization had a strategic commitment to their existing system and had no interest in switching. We had all been fooled by our own activity into thinking there was solid interest.

There are many things (good and bad) that can be learned from this experience, but the element I want to point out is that when we look at activities from our side—the demos, the proposal, the agreement—this opportunity appeared to be progressing wonderfully, and we were fooled by that. We must always remember that despite our sales cycle, the buyer has their own buying cycle. Ignoring their buying cycle and focusing only on the steps of your sales cycle may cause you to invest your time unwisely.

Our rep had invested his time and the time of many support personnel doing months of demonstrations along with preparing proposals and legal work for a client who was basically just indulging him. None of the rep's activities asked the client to make any significant commitment in terms of action or energy beyond watching another dog-and-pony show. Had our rep used call objectives that were truly advances, he could have changed the course of the sale or determined earlier that the opportunity was not a good use of his time.

Ultimately, this inappropriate investment of time and energy caused a very good rep to miss not only his quarter, but also his year, in terms of quota.

I realize this is a dramatic example so I want to reiterate that over focusing on what *we* do as professionals rather than focusing on what the *client* does applies to all sales of all sizes with sale cycles that are both long and short.

It is important that we have a clear picture from our client's perspective as well as our own in order to assure mutual success. Henry Ford said it best, "If there is any one secret of success, it lies in the ability to get the other person's point of view and see things from his angle as well as your own."

I also want to mention here that our job as professionals is not to educate or give presentations. Both of those are merely a means to an end. Our goal as professionals is to facilitate action on behalf of our clients.

Always remember that as professionals we don't get paid for the actions we take. We only get paid based on the actions our clients take. The action we facilitate for our clients improves their condition as well as our own in a virtuous win-win cycle.

"Our goal as professionals is to facilitate action on behalf of our clients."

Embrace your role as a leader and change agent. Your prospect is meeting with you because they want to improve in some way, and they are looking to you for guidance and leadership. Through your knowledge, skills, and facilitation you become the catalyst that empowers them to reach their goals.

The actions that will best improve a client's condition will vary from client to client and will change over time. This is why we need to have a clear understanding of what constitutes a win for each specific client and articulate that in our overall sales objective.

As for individual call objectives, in a generic sense, every sales encounter has the same goal—to get the prospective client to commit to an advance and move closer to their desired outcome. In this sense you are a coach helping them get from where they are to where they want to be.

> *"In a generic sense, every sales encounter has the same goal—to get the prospective client to commit to an advance."*

In a moment we will explore an entire range of advances from best to worst that you might possibly set as your call objective—so you have a targeted *ideal* advance as well as several fall-back advances if your ideal advance proves unrealistic.

The Three Magic Pre-call Questions

As we conclude this chapter I want to introduce you to the Three Magic Pre-call Questions. You should know the answer to each of these before going into any sales encounter. If you master the habit of answering these three questions before every sales encounter, you will find your effectiveness in sales magnified many times over. In fact, mastering this habit alone will make this book worth 10,000 times more than what you paid for it. So it's worth perfecting and incorporating into your daily activities.

Here are the Three Magic Pre-call Questions:

Prior to every sales encounter—whether in person, by phone, or otherwise—answer the following three questions:

1. Why should this client see me?

2. What do I want the client to do?

3. How can I provide value on this encounter?

Give this a try right now before proceeding. Look at your calendar, take your next five appointments, and for each appointment answer these three short questions on a piece of paper.

This is an important exercise, so really do it. You'll be glad you did. I'll be waiting for you here when you're done.

What did you discover? Was it easy, or did you find it challenging?

After getting this far into the book, most folks can do a decent job of answering the second question (though we will greatly improve on that shortly). However, all three questions can throw people for a loop. In the upcoming chapters, we will discuss each question individually with our main focus being the second question and briefly touching on questions one and three.

"Answering the three magic pre-call questions before each encounter will magnify your effectiveness many times over."

With these preliminaries under our belt we will be able to execute The Perfect Close to its maximum effectiveness.

Closing Secret #8 - By setting appropriate call objectives for each encounter we will achieve an unbroken chain of successful advances that will ultimately lead to closing the sale.

Conclusion

Call Objectives (pre-planned Advances) are a key part of maximizing the effectiveness of The Perfect Close. For that reason the next three chapters discuss the three magic pre-call questions in more detail. Having preplanned advances as your call objectives will multiply your effectiveness many times over. Planning your call does not need to be complicated. By answering the three magic questions you will be prepared to use The Perfect Close and further increase your effectiveness on each encounter.

In the next chapter we will explore how to answer one of the most important elements of your planning process – the answer to the first of the three magic pre-call questions: Why should this client see me?

CHAPTER 7

Why Should this Client See Me?

"The only person that can decide what is valuable...
is the customer."

–John Spence

The first of the Three Magic Pre-call Questions is "Why should this client meet with me?" Why should they spend even one minute talking with you?

The question gets right to the core of your value proposition. What is it about your offer that is of benefit to your client? Said another way, something you offer brings measurable value to your clients. What is that? The measurable value you bring to your clients is the reason they should meet with you. That is your Value Proposition.

I will be candid and say that it is embarrassingly common for salespeople and other professionals to not have a clear understanding of their value proposition and the value they bring to their clients. Unfortunately, your value proposition is mission-critical information that you must have in order to succeed in selling. So it is vital that you have a clear understanding and can articulate in a tangible way the value you bring.

"The measurable value you bring to your clients is the reason
they should meet with you. That is your Value Proposition."

Developing your value proposition is a large and important topic and beyond the scope of this book. In a future work I will discuss how to develop and best articulate your value proposition to clients. For now however, just in case you found yourself without a clear value proposition, I offer this short bit of coaching. If you are experienced in this area feel free to skip to the next chapter.

Communicating Your Value Proposition

A value proposition is the measurable value you deliver to your clients. This is the reason why they should do business with you. Most people tend to describe what they do rather than the value they bring. This is a big mistake, and it is critical to know how to articulate the real value you deliver.

Your value proposition communicates (among other things) both the measurable value you deliver, as well as how you differ from competitors or alternatives in your same space. Without a measurable value proposition it will be hard for you to command any kind of price for your solution because prospective clients have no discernible value to compare against your price. Without a value proposition your product or service simply looks like an additional cost.

Lack of a value proposition also tends to make all vendors look the same to buyers. Without a value proposition clients will assume that all solutions in the same space solve with roughly the same degree of effectiveness. How can they know otherwise?

So a strong value proposition is among the most important things you can develop for your business.

> *"A strong value proposition is among the most important things you can develop for your business."*

A basic value proposition has three core components:

1. A Metric

2. A Direction

3. Magnitude

Metrics - The metric component is the name attached to the area(s) you improve. All businesses have them. Sometimes they are formalized, and sometimes they are not. It answers the question "How do you measure whether or not you are doing well in this area?"

Examples of formalized Metrics for Sales might include:

- Number of Units Sold

- Close Ratio

- Revenue Growth

- Lead Conversion Ratio

- Number of Opportunities

Examples of formalized Metrics for Accounts Receivable might include:

- Days Sales Outstanding (DSO)

- Percentage of AR over 60 Days

- Average Days Delinquent

- Bad Debt Percentage

- Operating Cost per Transaction

Every industry has their formalized metrics for measuring performance. What are the formalized metrics for measuring performance for your clients?

Sometimes metrics are less formal than the above examples, but rest assured they are still there. Very often, they are simply measured in terms of time, money, counts, ratios, or percentages. Other times the metric will be something unique to that customer alone.

Some examples might be:

- Time to Complete [something]

- Customer Satisfaction

- Acceptance Rate

- Positive Comments

- Usability

- Quality

"Every industry has their formalized metrics for measuring performance."

Again, a full treatment of how to develop value propositions is beyond the scope of this book, but you can discover the metric(s) your clients use to measure performance by asking these questions:

- "What tells you when you are doing well in this area?"

- "What tells you if something is going wrong?"

- "What suggests to you that you could be doing better in this area?"

With metrics you are simply looking for the means by which they measure results (good or bad). When you use a client's metrics in your value proposition you are speaking their lingo and communicating on a level they immediately understand. Simply using their terms will increase both your value and your credibility.

Direction - Direction is simple. It answers the question, "What is happening to the value of this Metric?" Is it going up or down? Depending on the context, either one might be good. We want Sales Revenue to go up, and we want Material Costs to go down—both of these are good.

Magnitude - Lastly we have magnitude. Magnitude answers "How much...?" That is, how much is the metric going up or down? What is the actual value of the change? Did it go up or down by a percentage? Was it reduced by a fixed amount? What is the quantified level of improvement?

Putting Your Value Proposition Together

With these three components you have the minimum you need to craft a value proposition. The components can be arranged in various ways to maximize clarity and impact. Here is a basic formula and example:

Formula: [Direction] + [Metric] + [Magnitude]

Example: We increase lead conversion by an average of 47%.

> *"When you use a client's metrics in your value proposition you are speaking their lingo and communicating on a level they immediately understand."*

Direction + Metric + Magnitude = Value Proposition

This is the bare minimum. There are many other elements that go into creating an effective value proposition such as target statements and impacts. You should have a value proposition for all of your solutions and services so you can speak confidently about the value each one brings. Additionally, you will probably need a more generalized value proposition that encompasses everything your business offers.

With your value proposition(s) crafted you should be able to easily define a legitimate business reason to meet with your prospective client. That's your answer to, "Why should this client see me?"

Now, work this into a complete sentence for your sales encounter and include what you know about the client's current situation. Here's an example:

Question: Why should this client see me?

Answer: This client should see me because with their new expansion it is likely I can reduce their human resource costs as much as 19% using automation.

Closing Secret #9 - Your value proposition is mission-critical information that you must have in order to succeed in selling.

Conclusion

Your Value Proposition communicates the tangible results you produce for your clients. It differentiates you from competitors and alternatives. Your value proposition also justifies your pricing.

Creating a value proposition for your business as well as for each of your solutions represents foundational work that must take place before value can be communicated in any form of messaging.

It is important that you are clear about the value you bring prior to any sales call or encounter. Your value proposition answers the question "Why should this client see me?" in a compelling and tangible way. Clarity in your value proposition will magnify your value and your credibility with prospective clients. It will also direct and accelerate your conversations with clients right to the core reasons for doing business with you.

In the next chapter we will discuss how to answer the second of the three magic pre-call questions: What do I want the client to do?

James Muir

CHAPTER 8

What Do I Want My Prospective Client to Do?

"There are a lot of smaller 'asks' that you need to make on your way to the final 'ask.' You can't move the final 'ask' forward by skipping the 'asks' that should have come before it."

–Anthony Iannarino

The answer to the question "What do I want my client to do?" is the basis of your call objective—the advance you want to happen as a result of this encounter. It is the action you want them to take. Each advance will incrementally bring you and your client to an arrangement that benefits you both.

You already understand what an advance is and that it requires both action and energy on behalf of your prospect. What we will do now is expand on that concept to help you develop a range of possible advances for all of your sales encounters. By doing this, you will have an *ideal* advance to work toward as your call objective as well as several *fall-back* advances if your ideal advance proves unrealistic for some reason.

Ideal Advance - the highest level of commitment you can reasonably expect your prospect to make as a result of this encounter.

Ultimately, the ideal advance on any given sales encounter would be to close the business. However, as previously mentioned, that is rarely a reasonable outcome in a complex sales process that involves more than one call. For that reason, we will be aiming for the highest level of incremental commitment we can realistically achieve. With that in mind, let's dig a little deeper into what makes an ideal advance.

There will generally be a number of potential actions that a prospect can take to move the sale forward. What we want to do is make the most of our time and the prospect's time by facilitating the largest incremental commitment appropriate at this juncture. To do that we will need to evaluate our possible advances against each other. The four criteria of call objectives will make that easier.

Your call objectives should meet four criteria:

1. They should be specific and measurable.

2. They should center on the action the prospect will take.

3. They should move the sale forward.

4. They should be reasonable from the prospect's perspective.

Specific and measurable - Just like your sales objectives, your call objectives should also be specific and measurable. In the case of call objectives it is considerably easier because we are looking for tangible evidence that the action took place. It is simply an action or commitment made by your prospect. So it either happened or it didn't. Changes in attitude or feeling are challenging to measure. So instead, look for *actions* that actually demonstrate their change in attitude or feeling. As you brainstorm advances ask yourself, "What actions demonstrate a change (or confirmation) of attitude or feeling?"

<u>Center on the action the prospect will take</u> - We've covered this already but it bears repeating. Call objectives are about what we want the *prospect* to do—not what *you* do. As we brainstorm all the possible advances, remember to focus on actions your prospect could take as a result of your meeting. Ask yourself, "What action could my prospect take to advance the sale forward?"

<u>Move the sale forward</u> - Each advance should incrementally progress the sale toward ultimate completion. Depending on circumstances, there may be many increments or just a few. The key here is that, at the minimum, each action should add some sort of momentum to the sales process. Not all actions taken by the prospect will move the sale forward. Meetings, in and of themselves for example, neither move the sale forward nor backward. They are neutral. What happens as a result of the meeting may advance your sale, but the meeting itself (unless it requires a good deal of sacrifice on behalf of the prospect) is simply an opportunity.

When the Next Step Involves Your Competition

Ironically, sometimes the next big step in a prospect's evaluation process is to evaluate alternative solutions. While this may not be the advance we would generally seek, if the prospect is truly going to evaluate other alternatives, then our sale may be stalled until that step can take place. Understand and embrace the fact that evaluating alternatives is a key part of our prospect's buying process. Rather than fight this—help them with it.

You don't need to schedule your competition's presentation— that's going too far. However if a prospect is considering using their own internal resources to solve a problem, I have found it helpful to facilitate an internal meeting to evaluate the scope and practicality of an internal solution—because the opportunity will be stalled until they complete their evaluation of alternatives. You may never have to do this, but it does illustrate how to take into account your prospect's evaluation process and planning your advances around that.

Another thing to consider is that not all alternatives will involve direct competition. Clients may choose to buy a solution or service to solve a problem or they may consider solutions that don't involve buying anything. They may outsource an entire function or choose to stop doing a line of business for example.

You should anticipate that your prospective client will evaluate all possible alternatives to purchasing a solution and be prepared to discuss and facilitate the pros and cons of each one. Each time you help a client eliminate an alternative you are adding momentum and advancing your opportunity.

Having said this, you will find that there are many ingenious actions your prospect can take shy of involving alternative solutions that will keep the momentum of your sale moving forward.

Be reasonable from the prospect's perspective - As you brainstorm your potential advances, your list of possible prospect actions should range from simple to almost impossible. I once had a rep suggest that an entire client site attend a national user's conference. While this was an excellent thought exercise, it was completely impractical for the client to shut down operations for a week so their entire group could attend our user's conference. Still, once we pared it down to a reasonable scope, this was an excellent suggestion for advancing the sale. In the end, a dozen of their staff attended the conference, and it contributed to garnering a multi-million dollar account.

Advances vs. Engagement

In my workshops I have discovered that there are a number of interactions with a possible client that are generally positive but do not technically qualify as advances because they don't represent commitment, or they lack the sufficient energy required to be considered advances. Workshop attendees often get tripped up by these. To help protect you from this pitfall before brainstorming possible advances we should understand the difference between an *advance* and what I deem *Engagement* or to differentiate it with the same term as used in marketing—Sales Engagement.

Sales Engagement - interest that does not involve obligation.

This practical definition gives us a useful way to differentiate between an advance and what is simply curiosity or interest on behalf of a client.

An advance involves a commitment or obligation of some kind, yet there are many interactions with clients that don't involve commitments or obligations, but do demonstrate genuine curiosity and interest.

"Sales Engagement – Interest that does not involve obligation."

One way to approach engagement versus an advance is to consider them on a priority scale, where on one end *engagement* represents items that are of interest but not yet enough of a priority to invest time and energy, while on the other end of the spectrum you have advances which are of high enough priority to take action on.

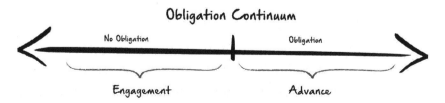

Obligation Continuum

This helps to gauge:

1. The prospective client's level of commitment.

2. The best possible advance to suggest at this moment in time.

This allows you to make the best use of both the prospect's time as well as your own.

The trap I repeatedly see professionals fall into is wasting huge amounts of time on prospective business that will never close because they have misjudged curiosity and interest (and sometimes simple politeness) as indicators of good sales opportunities. Curiosity and interest are nice, but we don't want to make it more than it is—and we certainly don't want to invest our most valuable resource (time) without a reasonable assurance of a positive outcome.

With that backdrop, let's explore some of the most common indicators of engagement that are often confused for advances.

- **Prospect asks you for a proposal.** This is probably the engagement most commonly mistaken as an advance. Prospects are curious and very much want to know the prices. You should expect them to ask for a proposal. In fact, it would probably be better to think of *not* getting a request for a proposal as a bad sign rather than to think of the request as an advance.

  The problem with a proposal request (the price) is that it doesn't require any energy or commitment on behalf of the prospect, so it's an easy matter for them to request it.

  I strongly recommend that you wait for the prospect to request the proposal rather than you suggesting it. Prospects will rarely refuse your suggestion to give them a proposal. Also, if you ask, you lose what can be achieved by observing the moment they decide to ask. Be patient, they will ask. And when they ask, the context will tell you a little something about where they are in the sales process. If you volunteer it, however, you will know nothing because even disinterested prospects are curious enough to want to know the price.

Often, prospects will request proposals before it is appropriate. In complex sales, there may be many prerequisites involved before a proposal can be generated.

As you can see, a request for proposal is a small sign of engagement—not an advance. The best path, if you can, is to upgrade the prospect's request to an advance by requiring something logical of them that represents a commitment or an expenditure of energy such as an assessment or detailed discovery before you produce the proposal.

- **Prospect asks questions regarding the proposal or solution.** Asking specific, detailed questions about the proposal or solution is indeed a good sign of engagement. You can very often tell by the quality of their questions how interested they are and how much homework they have done prior to your meeting. Interest is not commitment, however. Use the information you glean from their questions to suggest a logical advance that will move the process incrementally forward as well as test their commitment to the process.

- **Sending a proposal.** Sending a proposal is not an advance. It may be a step. It is definitely engagement, but it is not an advance.

Probably the biggest crime in selling is to just email a proposal to a prospective client. Emailing a proposal and expecting the prospect to understand it without any assistance is shirking your responsibility as a facilitator. It's also a bad idea.

When you email your proposal you lose the opportunity to 1. Review, clarify, and confirm with the prospect the accuracy of the proposed solution, 2. Collaborate with the prospect to make the proposal perhaps bigger or even more ideal, 3. Discuss with your contact the dynamics around what will happen next, and 4. Further develop your relationship with the prospect.

A common ailment reported by those who confess to simply emailing proposals is that often the prospect stops responding to calls and messages. This is because there is no value inherent in your *interaction* (which we will cover in the next chapter). If you are not adding value or insight to every interaction, after the prospect has your proposal they may decide they have everything of value that you can offer, and then they will only reach out to you on their terms.

Rather than emailing your proposal (or sending it FedEx), schedule a meeting to review your proposal with them.

- **Read or study a copy of your presentation or supporting material.** When a prospect invests significant time and energy in reviewing your presentation or supporting material, it is a positive sign representing worthwhile engagement and possibly an advance. The challenge is in deciphering how much time and energy the prospect actually invested in reviewing your materials. If you can tell by their questions and comments that they have truly pored over your materials, great! They have demonstrated engagement. But unfortunately, it is far more frequent that the prospect requests these documents (or simply accepts them if you suggested it) and never actually does anything with it.

The best approach here is to turn their interest into a meeting or conversation and suggest a logical advance as an outcome of that.

- **One of their personnel contacts you to gather additional information (IT, engineers, managers, supervisors).** You should be encouraged if a member of your potential client's staff contacts you out of the blue to gather additional information. While not always true, this most likely indicates that an advance has taken place internally, without your knowledge. These requests come from someone who will likely be affected by the decision. That doesn't mean they necessarily support you or the decision being made, but it definitely represents engagement.

This person is already expending energy by calling you. We are just unsure of their commitment level. The best approach here is to engage the person in healthy dialogue about their role in the process, their feelings about the project, and the dynamics around the decision. The context of their answers will usually tell you if they are friend or foe. You can convert this interaction into an advance by being super helpful and committing them to one of your advances (e.g., gathering agenda items for a group meeting, reference client visit, etc.).

- **Request help in explaining an area related to the sale to another person.** It's a good thing when a prospect requests coaching from you regarding how to present your solution to others. This is engagement that foreshadows a possible advance.

The best approach here is to first discuss with your prospect the dynamics of the situation. Understand what they are trying to accomplish and assess the best way of accomplishing that for them. The biggest challenge for you is that your contact is not likely to articulate the value of your solution better than you, so unless their internal politics dictate otherwise, you are far better served delivering the explanation yourself rather than having your contact or someone else inside their company be an agent for you. Upgrade this engagement to an advance, if possible, by scheduling the discussion to happen with you directly.

- **Attends a webinar or watches an on-line demo on your website.** When a prospect, or someone within their organization, attends one of your webinars, watches an online video demo, or performs another similar activity it demonstrates a good level of engagement. These are information-gathering activities and generally don't require a high level of energy or commitment. Be aware, however, these activities could also be antagonistic toward you as the person may be using these means to gather information against the project. Also, if these things happen toward the end of your sales cycle, it may be an indicator that the prospect is not as far along as you thought.

  The best course of action is to contact the person within the organization who took these actions and engage them further to understand their motives. Learn the situation and the dynamics involved, and then with that knowledge, suggest one of your advances.

- **Refers another prospective client to you.** In most cases this shows a very high, positive level of engagement. If they have already contacted the prospective referral, had a discussion, and followed-through with the referral, then you have an advance. Congratulations! If on the other hand, they are simply dropping the name of a possible prospect, you need to dig a little deeper.

Discover the details behind their relationship with the referral and understand why they are making the suggestion. Then, if possible, upgrade this engagement to an advance by asking if they are willing to make an introduction for you.

Understanding the difference between an advance and engagement is an important part of continuing momentum in your opportunities. With The Perfect Close you are going to suggest an advance. It is important then that the actions we suggest genuinely progress the opportunity and move the client toward their goals. You now know how to avoid the most common engagements mistaken for advances. With that under your belt it's time to brainstorm possible advances for your type of sale.

Brainstorming Advances

We are now going to brainstorm some possible advances for your type of sale. This is a critical exercise because these advances will form the basis of the questions you will ask using The Perfect Close. The strategy is to give yourself a wide range of possible actions that your prospective client might take.

Before we start, let me note that every sale is unique and advances that work wonderfully for one opportunity might be inappropriate for another. In fact, to the degree that you are tailoring your advances for a given opportunity it is a good sign that you are genuinely engaging your prospect at a higher level. So, this exercise should be performed before each sales encounter to help you think through the best possible outcome for that prospect at that time. For now we will be performing this exercise in a generic sense for all opportunities.

You'll find that given your particular type of sale, there will be a pattern to the kinds of advances you can reliably request with positive results. Brainstorming those now will speed the process for you in the future and possibly help you discover some advances that you may not have considered before.

To facilitate comparison we will use a table to compile and prioritize ideas. If you are on a sales team this exercise is best done as a group where you can brainstorm together and bounce ideas off each other. On a whiteboard or a sheet of paper draft some headers like the ones below, or go to PureMuir.com and download the online form for this exercise.

Possible Advance / Client Action	Measured By	Impact	Achievability / Reasonable	Best Choice / Priority

The form is simple. Here's how to use it:

Step 1 - In the **Possible Advance/Client Action** column, brainstorm together and write down all the possible actions that your prospects could take. Ignore the columns to the right for now. Just get out all the ideas you can. This is a brainstorm. Further along, I will point you toward a resource to trigger additional ideas, but first, start with your own. Write down as many as you can. Keep going until you run out of gas. Then, move on to step 2.

Step 2 - Review your ideas. Then, in the **Measured by?** column, discuss and write down how you will know when this action has taken place.

This will help you discern advances from engagement or mere feelings.

Step 3 - Under the **Impact** column, discuss and rate how impactful this advance would be on the development of your sale. Rate as High, Medium, Low, or None. This will help identify your most ideal advances.

Step 4 - For the **Achievability/Reasonable** column, as a group, rate the achievability/reasonableness of each advance on a scale of 1 to 5 (1=very difficult; 5=easy to achieve). This step will help you assess how realistic each advance is from your client's perspective. This will change from opportunity to opportunity, but for now we will just be thinking in the generic sense.

Your table should look similar to the abbreviated one below:

Possible Advance / Client Action	Measured By	Impact	Achievability / Reasonable	Best Choice / Priority
Get introduced to executive management	Introduction takes place	High	4	
Agree to do assessment & share financials	Shares financials, schedules assessment	High	2	
Arrange meeting with technical team to discuss requirements/options	Technical meeting takes place	Medium	3	
Meet with reference account	Reference account meeting takes place	Medium	3	
Schedule demonstration	Demonstration takes place	Low	5	

Step 5 - If you were planning for an actual meeting you would prioritize each advance and list them by priority in your encounter plan. For now we are simply brainstorming so you can leave the **Best Choice/ Priority** column blank. Note: You will learn more about encounter plans in Chapter 10.

Building On Your Possible Advances

Many find this exercise quite illuminating, and no doubt you discovered some patterns to the advances and action steps that you most often use. From there we can build on that. You will find forms for this exercise and additional ideas for advancing your sales available free for download at PureMuir.com.

The best salespeople are able to get prospects to agree to a continuous stream of small actions. I am often amazed at some of the ingenious actions forged from the creativity of these skilled professionals. They always have an *ideal* advance as well as an array of alternate actions to propose. This increases the likelihood that each encounter will end with one or more advances.

> *"The best salespeople are able to get prospects to agree to a continuous stream of small actions."*

Tips on Strengthening Your Advances

As we wrap up this section on advances I want to offer a few tips you can use to make your advances even stronger and more effective. You will find that by simply tweaking your advances, you can increase their effectiveness to a large degree.

Make your interaction as direct and personal as possible. Efficient is not always effective. With the advent of the internet there are many ways to interact with your prospects and clients that do not involve face-to-face contact (e.g., email, internet presentations, conference calls, etc.).

For many applications these are efficient and time-saving approaches, so use them when appropriate. However, communication, understanding, and the development of relationships are all maximized in face-to-face interactions. You cannot detect facial cues on conference calls and internet presentations.

To the degree that you can be directly engaged in personal, face-to-face interactions with your prospects, the strength and effectiveness of your advances will be improved. In-person, face-to-face interactions are the best.

Pick the best possible location for your meeting. Where you meet can greatly change the dynamic of the meeting. Location can make a meeting more or less effective to a very large degree. How the venue affects the outcome of a meeting is situational and requires some consideration. There are no hard and fast rules, but consider the setting for each of the following:

- *Reference Client Site* - If you can arrange your meeting with a prospective client to take place at an existing client's location (aka reference client), odds are the effectiveness of your meeting will greatly increase. This environment will be oozing social proof and your prospect will have direct access to an existing client for third-party validation of your solution.

- *Event or Show* - This can help or hurt depending on circumstances. Trade shows can be convenient for prospects, but one of the logistics that make it convenient is the proximity of competitors and alternate choices. Trade shows also present many potential distractions. Nevertheless, such events often create excitement and high energy levels that can be motivating for your prospective clients. If it is your own event (such as a user-group meeting), then you have a meeting trifecta: heightened energy, access to your top personnel, and social proof all around you. If you do use a company event or trade show to conduct a meeting, plan it carefully so that distractions are minimized during the actual time you meet.

• *Your Corporate Office* - Having your prospective client visit your office or headquarters is a great way to showcase the leadership of your management team as well as the talent of your technical, implementation, and support teams. Meeting at your corporate office will help address questions regarding your company's credibility, competency, or capabilities to solve or execute the solution. A well-choreographed visit to your office or headquarters can strengthen your advance significantly.

• *The Prospective Client's Site* - Meeting at the prospect's location is far stronger than an internet-based meeting or phone conference. Moving from a virtual meeting to an actual on-site meeting will greatly strengthen both an engagement and an advance. It is important to remember, however, that a prospect's site may also come with potential interruptions. If interruptions are a real possibility, then it may make sense to shoot for a meeting off-site.

• *Off-site Location* - The primary benefit of off-site meeting locations is to eliminate interruptions and allow prospective clients to focus better on your message and the task at hand. Off-site meetings vary wildly in their scope and effectiveness. A dedicated retreat to an out-of-country destination can create maximum focus but may not be practical. On the other hand, a simple lunch or dinner off site can be a mixed bag—sometimes good, sometimes not. It's worth noting that going off site does have limitations. The opportunity to add additional parties or explore their premises is eliminated. Sometimes you can accomplish an on-site and off-site meeting in the same encounter (e.g., a tour of their premises and then a lunch meeting). It is important to plan your off-site meetings strategically. When executed well, off-site locations can improve the quality of your meeting.

Add valuable people to your meeting. The involvement of key people either from your company or the prospect's company can strengthen your meeting (which may be an advance in itself) as well as the action items and advances that result from it. This could include key decision makers, technical resources, domain experts, or even existing clients.

Add value to every interaction. Strengthen every encounter by adding value in some way. By making each meeting inherently worthwhile, you train your prospects and clients to value every interaction with you. There are many ways to achieve this. This is the subject of our next chapter.

Additional Resources

If you are interested in creating even more advances for your call objectives download the forms and ideas for advancing the sale document at PureMuir.com. There you will find many additional ideas on how to develop effective advances for your type of sale.

Closing Secret #10 - By brainstorming we can plan the ideal advance as well as alternate/additional advances for our sales encounter.

Conclusion

Complex sales are like a flywheel, and each time we obtain an advance from a prospect the flywheel gains momentum. Some sales require many pushes on the flywheel and others just a few. By brainstorming and planning ahead we can choose the *ideal* advance for our interaction and have a number of alternative advances in the event our primary call objective proves unrealistic.

Your *ideal advance* is the highest-level commitment that you can appropriately and reasonably expect your prospect to make as a result of this encounter.

Each successful advance adds momentum to your sale's flywheel and brings your client closer to their goal. As mentioned previously, planning your call is one of the biggest factors in sales success. Next up we will outline step-by-step how to plan your calls to deliver value and advance the sale.

CHAPTER 9

How Can I Provide Value on This Encounter?

"Value doesn't happen by accident. It is the result of deliberate planning and preparation."

–Andy Paul

We have answered two of the Three Magic Pre-call Questions:

- Why should this client see me?

- What do I want the client to do?

And now, we turn to the third of these three important questions, "How can I add value on this encounter?"

It is critical that we add value on every single sales encounter. This is a relatively new development in selling. Twenty years ago it was not as important that salespeople deliver anything beyond information about their products and services. Because of the Internet all of that has changed. It is now vital that we make the sales experience itself valuable for clients.

"It is critical that we add value on every single sales encounter."

There are numerous ways to add value. If we included every possible permutation, the count would probably be infinite. Covering everything within the pages of this book is impossible, but what follows reveals why customers expect value along with helpful guidelines, tips, and suggestions on how to add value on every sales encounter.

The Disappearing Sales Process

Many industry experts predict that the need for salespeople will be dramatically reduced in coming years. Gartner Research for example predicts that by 2020, 85% of interactions between businesses will be executed without human intervention.[1] That would mean a massive reduction in the millions of salespeople worldwide.

Research conducted by the Corporate Executive Board (CEB)[2] reveals that on average customers have completed 57% of their buying process before they ever contact a salesperson. This is a game-changing dynamic for sales professionals and one to which salespeople worldwide are still adjusting.

The driver behind this change is the Internet. The worldwide web has made it possible for customers to thoroughly research options long before ever needing to reach out to a salesperson. Search engines locate exactly what clients are looking for in fractions of a second. And, thanks to very sophisticated algorithms, most of the vital information is likely to be contained in the first few pages of results.

The impact of this change compared to the earlier sales era is that, for the most part, buyers no longer need salespeople to provide product information. Without any need to contact a salesperson, buyers can now put together a very clear picture of options in a very short period of time. In fact, if a buyer has a propensity to seek the lowest price they can often let their fingers do the walking and never see a salesperson at all.

So buyer's now have two options:

1. Bypass a salesperson and do business transactionally, or

2. Engage a sales professional to derive value from the sales experience itself.

As we move into the future and the Internet provides information and simplifies the process to purchase even more complex solutions transactionally, more and more purchasers will be choosing option number one. This is the driver behind Gartner's prediction.

However, the remainder of buyers who choose to engage a sales professional want to receive added value from the sales process itself. This has raised the bar of expectation of what salespeople should deliver throughout the sales experience.

It would be hard to overstate the impact of this new dynamic. Delivering value on each and every sales encounter is about staying relevant to the buyer. Without it, they no longer need you. So we must make it an imperative to add value on every sales interaction.

Closing Secret #11 - Every sales interaction must be inherently valuable.

You Are the Biggest Factor

Many studies have been done over the years to examine which sales factors are most influential in the buying process. Two of the most noteworthy and extensive come from HR Chally and Corporate Executive Board (CEB). They spanned more than two decades and exceeded 100,000 interviews. They examined many factors including company and brand, quality of offering, total solution, total value, the salesperson, and price to determine which of these have the most influence in purchase decisions.

Both studies agree that far and away the most influential factor is the salesperson. In fact, the salesperson is two to four times more important than any other factor.[3]

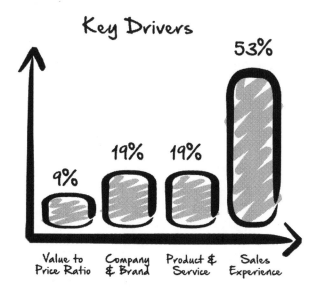

Key Drivers in Customer Loyalty Source: CEB 2012

I'd like to accentuate three conclusions from this data:

1. You cannot rely solely on your solution, your brand, or price. You are the number one influence.

2. You have far more control and influence than you may have previously realized. How you sell matters more than anything else.

3. This can work for you or against you.

For these reasons it is absolutely critical that each and every experience with prospective clients be enjoyable and have inherent value. If you deliver a valuable and enjoyable experience in every encounter, prospects will extrapolate that their experience after the sale will also be valuable and enjoyable.

This is an extremely strong sales dynamic, and you can now see the importance of *consistently* adding value to each and every encounter. Imagine how much more effective you can be by carefully and thoughtfully planning out each experience with your prospects.

We cannot afford to have any *samples* that are sub-par during our prospect's sales experience.

Training Your Client

By consistently delivering value on each and every encounter we train our prospects to see us as something more than just the agent who happens to offer a given solution. They see us as valuable assets, domain experts, trusted advisors, and precious resources who can help them achieve the outcomes they desire.

When buyers see you in this way:

- They will share more information with you.

- They will ask for advice and accept your recommendations.

- They will refer you to others.

- They will forgive your mistakes.

- They will protect and warn you.

- You will increase your sales both in number and dollar volume.

According to research done by Cahners, *Trusted Advisors* are 69% more likely to come away with the sale.[4] There are two keys to becoming a trusted advisor:

1. Value - Delivering what the client considers to be genuine value, and

2. Consistency - Delivering value in every experience with the client.

Extrapolation Bias

When you consider all the dimensions of a product or service, in most cases buyers spend a surprisingly small amount of time evaluating choices. This is especially true for the most complex solutions. It is also why trust, rapport, and good intent are so important in the sales process. The more complex a solution is, the more buyers rely on trust and outside validation. They realize they can never fully assess all the proportions of the solution, and so they utilize these as shortcuts (heavily in some cases) in their consideration of alternatives.

Have you ever lost a sale to a competitor whose offering was clearly inferior? There is a phenomenon that explains one of the reasons why this happens.

How you sell is a sample of how you solve.

Closing Secret #12 - How you sell is a sample of how you solve.

The time a prospect spends with a salesperson before the sale is an indicator of their experience after the sale. Each interaction with you is a "sample." Prospects are sampling their experience with you as much as they are evaluating the product or deliverable. In many cases (with service offerings especially) the experience during the sale is weighted far above the product itself or the methodology used.

This experience sample, because it is relatively small, makes clients prone to a cognitive bias known as *extrapolation bias*—a form of availability bias where we overestimate probabilities of events associated with memorable or dramatic occurrences.

With extrapolation bias we extrapolate what future events will become based upon a narrow sampling of current events. For example, if a stock is going up we may extrapolate that it will continue to go up. Or if our experience at a restaurant is good, we extrapolate that it will always be good.

Cognitive Biases

Cognitive biases are flaws in judgment caused by memory, social attribution, or statistical errors. Cognitive biases are a fascinating field, and I highly recommend studying them. They are simultaneously interesting and useful.

With this backdrop you can see how important each *sample* is during the sales process. In general, prospects will take the sum of their experiences with us and extrapolate them into what they think all future experiences will be. This can work for you or against you.

> *"Prospects will take the sum of their experiences with us and extrapolate them into what they think all future experiences will be."*

How did you lose to a competitor that was clearly inferior? Your prospect's narrow sampling from your competitor may have been exceptional while their sampling of you may have been sub-par. This is especially true with more complex solutions because prospects can never really get a sample adequate enough to fully understand all the dimensions of each offering—so they extrapolate.

If the prospect was not given enough opportunity to adequately sample each solution, they will extrapolate based on the narrow experience that they do have—and sometimes come to the wrong conclusion.

Again, this can work for you or against you. While we can do our best to give prospects a clear picture or sample of both our and the competitor's solutions, it is arguable that prospects can never really get a complete understanding until they have fully implemented and experienced the solution themselves. And then of course, it is already too late.

So how did you lose to a clearly inferior solution? Answer: You were outsold.

In professional selling we often hear that phrase, "You were outsold." Now, rather than taking this as a mindless quip or insult, you'll understand some of the mechanics actually involved.

When Clients Go Silent

A common complaint sellers have is when a prospect stops responding. While there are multiple causes for this, by far the greatest is that the prospect has come to the conclusion that the salesperson has nothing of value left to give them.

It's common for the prospective client to be responsive right up until the time they receive the proposal. Then, after they have the proposal, communication mysteriously stops. Most salespeople conclude that there is something wrong with the proposal or that the price is too high. Occasionally that can be the case, but in my experience it is not the primary cause.

The primary cause of a prospect going silent is that the sales agent has not been adding enough value throughout the sales process. Often, the salesperson has only been providing information about their products and services, and when we fail to provide any form of additional value, buyers assume this is all we're good for. As a consequence once they receive all the information about our solution that they need, they have no reason to continue engaging with us.

Typically, the final piece of information a prospect receives in our proposal is the price. Thus having received what they perceive to be the last useful piece of information, they cease communicating because they have no further use for us.

Are they wrong? Who can blame them? If we are not adding value beyond dispensing facts and pricing about our solution, then our prospects truly may have all the information they need and are doing exactly what they should be doing—maximizing their time.

The remedy to this problem is providing additional value to our prospects on each and every visit. And, as we will see in a moment, it must be more than just data and information.

When prospects learn that each and every encounter with you is valuable they will dialogue with you throughout their entire evaluation process and call upon you for the valuable insights you possess. In fact, this will continue long past the sales cycle. Clients will continue to engage you (in some cases even if you've moved on or left the industry) because of the value they know you bring and the respect they have for you. Additionally, if there does happen to be a challenge with your proposal or the price, they will reach out to you and provide the feedback you need to correct it.

The key is to make sure both clients and prospects see you as a valuable resource. By training them to see you as a trusted advisor and not just a person selling a product, prospects will buy and clients will return to you again and again.

One of my executive friends has a litmus test to determine whether or not a given salesperson is actually an established, trusted advisor. He observes their greeting when meeting with established clients. If the greeting is simply the obligatory, token acknowledgment he knows the salesperson is not of much value. On the other hand, if the exchange is more personal (e.g., a hug, a vigorous and joyful handshake) he knows they are a trusted advisor to that client. We should be striving to deliver enough value to elicit this kind of response from every client.

Clients Have Redefined Value

It used to be that clients most strongly valued our product information, our responsiveness when approached, our ability to fulfill an order or request, and our ability to provide the best offering and/or price. All of these are still very important, but since the advent of the Internet, buyers have redefined what value means to them during the sales cycle.

Revenue Storm recently surveyed B2B and B2C companies and pitted these two sets of values against each other to determine which set clients valued more:

- Value Category 1

  » Ability to fulfill an order or request

  » Ability to provide the best offering or price

  » Ability to respond and listen when approached

- Value Category 2

    » Ability to challenge current thinking

    » Ability to proactively bring innovative ideas

    » Ability to provide thought leadership

82% of respondents valued the items in Category 2 over the items in Category 1.

This is an amazing result and a harbinger of the value shift happening in the marketplace today. Elements like fulfillment, overall value, and responsiveness are critical and will always be an important part of the value equation, however, they have become expected. They are a minimum requirement to even get into the game. Momentum has shifted toward our ability to deliver insight and thought leadership, and buyers weight these values heavily when selecting a business partner.

What buyers seek today is insight. Let me illustrate with a personal story.

My youngest son Justin began having health issues at the age of eight while attending third grade. He was experiencing intermittent stomach pains and bouts of diarrhea. For months we tried all the standard remedies to no avail. We took him to physicians who employed their own series of treatments, also with no success.

During this period Justin developed an even worse symptom—severe depression. Every day, at home or at school, became emotionally taxing not only for him but also for those around him. I will be candid and confess that as a loving parent it was the most challenging and frustrating experience I have ever encountered. Each day promised a combination of physical pain, diarrhea, and emotional trial—and I was powerless to stop it. Often, I wished I could take his ailments upon myself so that he could experience relief.

Unfortunately, this continued for two years until Justin was finally diagnosed with Crohn's disease. By this time, however, it had become life-threatening. Justin was chronically dehydrated and anemic. He developed dark circles around his eyes, and the smallest exertion would completely deplete his energy. His skin became pale and yellow, and he developed sores around his mouth that refused to heal. He also developed insomnia, so he literally could get no respite from his condition. He would crawl into bed with my wife and me, and we would try our best to comfort him.

Sadness and frustration do not begin to describe my feelings as a parent during this time. But at least, finally, we had something—we had a solid diagnosis. Initially, I knew nothing of Crohn's disease, but with a desire to save my son's life I dove headlong into research and turned up thousands of pages of *contradictory* data on Crohn's disease. It was overwhelming. But it was my job, as Justin's loving father, to turn *data* into something valuable—*information and insight.*

In desperation I reviewed tremendous amounts of data. I organized the data and slowly distilled it into a coherent picture (information). I felt I understood Crohn's—what it was and how it worked. I had usable information now, but I was still missing something. I needed a clear path of what to do with my newfound knowledge. I needed *insight.*

Prospects and clients need the same. They have access to information, but what they need is *insight.* They want help understanding and designing a clear path that will lead them to their desired outcome.

Just as I sought, clients want the actionable steps that understanding the information provides.

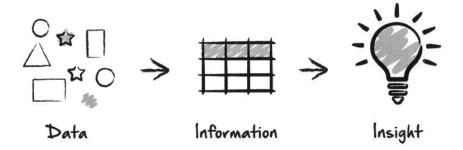

Data → Information → Insight

Ultimately, I identified a few individuals who shared with me practical insights on how we might treat Justin's condition in a non-steroidal, non-surgical way. Within a few months of administering this regimen, Justin recovered and remains in complete remission to this day.

I have tremendous respect and gratitude for these pioneering practitioners who helped me heal my son. I share this story with you because these are the same emotions—respect and gratitude—that you engender in your clients when you provide them with genuinely valuable insights.

Getting Help for IBS/IBD and Autoimmune Conditions

While the specific solutions we used to help my son is not relevant to this book, it is however, important to me that these valuable insights reach those suffering from this condition. If you have family, friends, or know anyone who suffers from IBS, IBD or another autoimmune condition, please reach out to me via my website at PureMuir.com via LinkedIn, or any other means. I will gladly help you. If I can save you the time I spent researching and the years of frustration we suffered, it will be well worth it.

What Makes Good Insight?

Three criteria make insight valuable:

1. It must be relevant.

2. It must be novel.

3. It must be actionable.

Relevant - Relevance is both subjective and contextual. It is subjective because what is relevant to one person may not be relevant to another—one person's signal is another person's noise. At the same time, relevance is contextual. What proves to be a valuable insight affecting the business as a whole may not be very valuable to the janitor who is not greatly affected by it.

It doesn't matter how valuable you feel your insight is. It only matters if the person you are talking to finds it relevant in their current context. Your prospect is the judge—not you.

Novel - The insight you share must provide something new—something that is not already known. Again, this is subjective. What you know may be very different from what your prospect knows. New information to you may be old information to them and vice versa. As the Huthwaite study proves, clients find new insights regarding problems, solutions, and opportunities very valuable indeed. So much so, that they are willing to pay a premium for the solutions related to them.

Actionable - The insight you share must be actionable—something they can do something about. If it doesn't suggest an action they can take, your client won't find it useful. Ideally, the insight you share will suggest something actionable that relates to the solution you provide.

While much more could be said about delivering insight, the basic formula for what makes good insight is:

$$Relevant + Novel + Actionable = Good\ Insight$$

What Customers Value Most

As mentioned, buyers have two basic options, 1. Skip the salesperson by researching solutions themselves and purchase everything transactionally, or 2. Derive value from the sales experience itself.

The ability to instantly research and compare solutions via the Internet is rapidly commoditizing most industries. This means salespeople who are unable to add value to the sales experience won't have much to differentiate with beyond price.

Fortunately, research has shown that buyers will forego price concerns when additional value is delivered by the sales process itself.

Research done by Huthwaite uncovered that buyers are willing to pay a premium under the following circumstances:

- The seller identified an *Unanticipated Solution* for the buyer's problems.

- The seller identified an *Unrecognized Problem* the buyer was experiencing.

- The seller identified an *Unseen Opportunity*.

- The seller acted as more than just a vendor of products and services but instead served as a *Broker of Strengths* (their term).

Under these conditions buyers were willing to pay more for the given solution.[5]

Take a look at the first three circumstances in this list. They all point to something that is new and unknown to the buyer. This is an important observation that helps us understand exactly what *insight* means and what makes it valuable to clients and prospects.

"Research has shown that buyers will forego price concerns when additional value is delivered by the sales process itself."

Practical Tips on Adding Value to Every Encounter

It's easy to say that you should add value to every encounter, but it's quite another to offer you concrete ways of how to actually go about doing that. The remainder of this chapter does just that. Read on for suggestions on how you can add value to each and every encounter.

The Most Common Mistake to Avoid

It's a cardinal sin to meet with a prospect or client with no defined purpose. In fact, each meeting should have at least two purposes:

1. A compelling business reason—your answer to "Why should this client see me?"

2. A plan to deliver added value.

Without a defined purpose you are wasting their time (as well as your own). If you are "just checking in" or "touching base," stop it. Nothing telegraphs that you have nothing valuable to offer or that you really only care about them purchasing something than an encounter with no purpose (e.g., "just checking in" or "touching base"). When you do this, you're just praying the time is right for them to buy. Since that's the case, why not just say so, "Hey Bob, are you going to buy something already or not?" Because your client knows the real reason you are contacting them.

Let me share a story. Decades ago in my first few months as a field salesperson I conducted a seminar to present our solution. After a fairly in-depth demonstration one particular attendee was engaged and asked for a proposal. Being new and inexperienced I excitedly crafted a proposal and faxed it to her (you're right, I've already made a dozen mistakes in this scenario, but that's not the point).

Not surprisingly she didn't contact me with any questions, so I reached out to see if I could answer her questions. Nope. She didn't have any. It all made sense to them. Not knowing what to say next I muttered something like, "Well, call me if you have any questions." Again, not surprisingly, no call came.

Being new I asked my boss what I should do next. His reply was, "Call them and see if they are ready to buy." This was some bad advice, but being new, I did as he suggested. I called her and in a wishy-washy way asked if they were ready to buy. Nope. Not ready yet.

Before I tell you what happened next, I have to disclose how nice and sweet my contact at the account was. I think she recognized my inexperience, so she was incredibly tolerant with my calls. She was truly a saint.

Monday's sales meeting comes around, and we look at the forecast. This account was still listed as an opportunity, so just like clockwork my boss's advice was to, "Call them and see if they are ready to buy." And I did—an amazing eight more times...

Each of these calls was about a week apart. My prospect probably began to expect them. And each time I was literally saying, "Are you ready to buy?"... "Are you ready to buy yet?"... "Hey, are you ready buy yet?"

To this day I cringe every time I think about it. Finally, in the sweetest way, my contact let me know that there was really no reason for me to call any more. They had decided to do something else. She was very kind, but you know what I discovered later? They actually hadn't done anything else. Nice as she was, she just couldn't handle any more of my pointless calls.

I am grateful to have learned this lesson so early in my sales career. Don't make the same mistake I did. Over and over again, I added zero value to their effort and with each call I essentially told them, "I just want your money."

Don't do it. Add value on every single encounter.

The Key to Adding Value is Preparation

Being thoughtful and deliberate about how you plan to deliver value before each meeting is the key to adding value on every encounter. Do not try to add value on-the-fly. That's winging it, and professionals do not wing it.

In an upcoming chapter I will introduce you to forms that you can use to help you prepare, but a good old piece of paper and pencil can do the job just as well. This process complements any of the sales methodologies out there you might already be using.

Know What Stage of the Buying Process Your Prospect is In

Buyers go through eight distinctive stages whenever making a purchase.

1. Unaware

2. Awareness

3. Define Problem

4. Consider Options

5. Evaluate Solutions

6. Justify Decision

7. Final Selection

8. Implementation

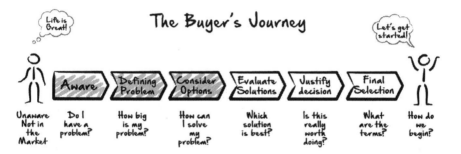

Buyers ask and gather answers that are distinctive to each stage. Knowing what stage your prospect is in prepares you to maximize the type of value you bring.

Consider the context of where your prospect is in their buying process. For example:

- If they are still only realizing that there is a need for change, then you might offer insight as to the gap between where they are and where they could be or should be.

- If they are aware of certain challenges but those problems are not crystallized in their minds, you might help them quantify the potential impact of their current problems or the upside with a particular opportunity.

- If they have quantified the upside potential, you might help them identify various options or tradeoffs to consider in order to achieve their desired outcome.

- If they are considering a few specific solutions, you might help them understand which are best matched to their desired results.

- If they have identified a particular path to achieve their goals, you might help them outline the plan or steps they need to take to reach their goal.

- If they are settled on a particular approach or solution, you might alert them to pitfalls to avoid and suggest ways to reduce risks associated with moving forward.

- If they are at the stage of finalizing their decision, you might share strategies to get executive approval and advise them on the most beneficial business model or terms.

- If they are preparing to implement a given solution or approach, you might recommend ways to leverage their new capabilities once the new solution is employed, and how to take their game to the next logical step.

There are infinite ways to add value at any stage of the buying cycle. The point is to be cognizant of where your prospect is, so you can offer the kind of value they will consider the most important at that stage.

It would be inappropriate or unwise to suggest a specific set of steps to implement a solution when your prospect hasn't yet quantified their challenge and determined whether it's worth addressing.

> *"There are infinite ways to add value at any stage of the buying cycle. Be cognizant of where your prospect is, so you can offer the kind of value they will consider the most important at that stage."*

To guide your thinking as you plan each encounter, ask yourself, "What stage of the buying cycle is my prospect/client in?" Then ask, "What would they consider most valuable at this stage?"

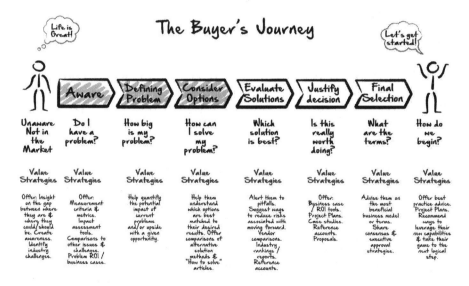

Use the buyer's stage to add unexpected value.

Make Your Agenda Surprisingly Valuable

It's important that your prospective client anticipate that their meeting with you will be valuable. The primary focus of the meeting should be the prospect's agenda. That means *their* stated interests, challenges, goals, etc.—not yours. "But what about this additional value I'm going to be adding?" you ask?

Be aware of these nuances when planning your meeting agenda:

1. The agenda should reflect their stated goals and interests as mentioned above. This is important above all else.

2. Your value-added component should be listed on the agenda as a general term or area. It **should not** be stated explicitly in the agenda.

You're thinking, "If I'm adding value to the meeting, shouldn't I be explicit about that value? Won't that increase their desire to meet and participate?"

There are times when you may want to define on the agenda the added value you intend to bring, however, cast your mind back to the Huthwaite research mentioned above where they determined the buyer's conditions for being willing to paying more:

- The seller identified an *Unanticipated Solution* for the buyer's problems.

- The seller identified an *Unrecognized Problem* the buyer was experiencing.

- The seller identified an *Unseen Opportunity*.

- The seller acted as more than just a vendor of products and services but instead served as a *Broker of Strengths*.

Recall that the first three on this list all point to something that is new and unknown to the prospect. This surprise factor is an important part of what makes these conditions impactful. I like to refer to this principle as *Unexpected Value*.

Unexpected Value - unanticipated value your prospect or client receives as a result of your meeting.

Being overt about the bonus value we intend to bring to the meeting telegraphs our value in advance and potentially diminishes the impact it will have during the meeting. So, we want to create a more generic description for the time in the agenda when we will be adding our surprise value.

Examples:

Instead of including this agenda item, "The 5 biggest pitfalls for executives, technical people, developers, and end-users" or "Solving the 5 biggest pitfalls." Include something like, "Top Challenges" or "Pitfalls."

Instead of, "Sample Implementation Plan." Use something like, "Execution," "Realization," or "Implementation."

These more general descriptions mask the surprise, concrete value you are going to deliver. Then, when you come to this agenda item, deliver the value you planned in full detail.

Do you see how each of these provides the opportunity in the agenda to insert *Unexpected Value* without telegraphing it in advance? This ensures that your unexpected value is a welcome surprise and carries more value. After all, doesn't everyone love a welcome surprise? For those involved in complex sales where many meetings occur, your clients and prospects will identify you, very quickly (sometimes after only two meetings), that you are a valuable source of knowledge and insight.

<u>Make Sure the Agenda Meets Their Expectations</u>

There's not much worse than the prospect feeling you have wasted their time because their expectation of what would be covered was not met.

This is a simple thing to avoid and will never happen when you are professional and prepared.

The key is to confirm your agenda with the client.

Make sure your agenda satisfies their expectation of what they want covered. Based on their input, create a proposed agenda and send it to them. Ask if there is anything else they would like to add. If there is, add it and reconfirm by sending a revised agenda. Then you can be sure you are both on the same wavelength. This alone will make your meeting more valuable.

It is unprofessional not to have an agenda. Not having an agenda sends the message that you are a time-waster not a value creator. It's easy to create an agenda so be professional and craft one for every encounter.

<u>Deliver Insight</u>

Delivering insight is the primary way you add value to each client encounter. There are nearly infinite ways to do this. Following is a list of ideas in various categories.

Prepare Powerful Questions

Your questions, in and of themselves, have an amazing capacity to create insight and bring value. Your ability to master questioning and facilitative dialogue is among the highest payoff skills. Mastering questioning would be a book unto itself, so what follows is a quick primer along with some helpful suggestions.

As a backdrop, questions that do not produce value are seen as a waste of time. The key criterion to a valuable question is that the answer provokes change for the better. When we ask questions that facilitate new understanding—how a prospect can improve their condition—they are deemed valuable.

Unfortunately, the most common questions are simply requests for information which do nothing to facilitate new understanding for the customer. While we must ask basic information-gathering questions from time to time, it is important to remember that prospects get no benefit from them. Since the prospect already knows the answer, the value is all one-sided—yours. Often, the answers to basic questions are found in the company's marketing collateral or website. Research in advance.

True value-adding questions are those to which the client does not already know the answer. They require thought, encourage reflection, advance the conversation into new territory, and the answers add value to the individuals involved.

"True value-adding questions are those to which the client does not already know the answer."

Stimulate Your Buyer's Thinking

There are two dimensions along which your questions stimulate thinking:

1. Knowledge
2. Cognitive

Knowledge Dimension

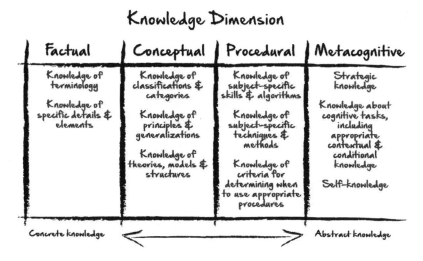

Factual	Conceptual	Procedural	Metacognitive
Knowledge of terminology Knowledge of specific details & elements	Knowledge of classifications & categories Knowledge of principles & generalizations Knowledge of theories, models & structures	Knowledge of subject-specific skills & algorithms Knowledge of subject-specific techniques & methods Knowledge of criteria for determining when to use appropriate procedures	Strategic knowledge Knowledge about cognitive tasks, including appropriate contextual & conditional knowledge Self-knowledge

Concrete knowledge ⟵——————⟶ Abstract knowledge

Knowledge - Your questions stimulate awareness along the knowledge dimension which spans from simple facts, to concepts, to processes, and then an awareness of their own knowledge of a given area.

In order to share knowledge it is important that you have some. How would you rate yourself on a scale of 1-10 in the subject matter area you are trying to sell? Commit yourself to becoming an expert in your field so you have a broad range of knowledge to draw upon when crafting your questions and facilitating understanding.

Cognitive Dimension

Remember	Understand	Apply	Analyze	Evaluate	Create
Identifying Recalling	Interpreting, clarifying, translating Illustrating, exemplifying Categorizing, classifying Summarizing, generalizing, abstracting Concluding, predicting, extrapolating, inferring Comparing, contrasting, matching Explaining, constructing models	Executing, carrying out Implementing, using	Differentiating, discriminating, distinguishing, focusing, selecting Organizing, finding coherence, integrating, parsing, structuring Attributing, deconstructing	Checking, coordinating, detecting, monitoring, testing Critiquing, judging	Generating, hypothesizing Planning, designing Producing, constructing

Lower order thinking ⟵——————————⟶ Higher order thinking

Cognitive - Your questions stimulate increasingly complex thinking along the cognitive dimension which spans from basic recall, to understanding, to applying the concept to themselves, to clearly analyzing and organizing the concept, to evaluating, differentiating, judging, and finally to creating their own designs based on the concept.

The further your questions are along these spectrums, the more value your buyer will perceive from your questions.

For example, along the knowledge spectrum, clients will not value questions that require them to rattle off a list of business facts as much as questions that require them to consider the steps they will take to achieve an outcome and where they are currently in that process.

Along the cognitive spectrum, buyers do not value questions that cause them to simply recall or understand concepts as much as they value questions that cause them to reflect, evaluate, and judge the details in a given area.

Unfortunately, the vast majority of questions in sales interactions are simply about facts and understanding—both along the lower end of the spectrums of these dimensions. That is not to say that facts and understanding are not important—they are. It's simply that those questions are not highly valued by prospects.

When we prompt higher-level thinking, we add value. Asking tough, powerful questions define you as a consultant and communicate your intent to genuinely help. This alone will add a great deal of value to each encounter and differentiate you from competitors.

Dynamics of High-Value Questions

It's important to note that in most cases higher level questions force clients to think in ways they haven't before. The "Ah-ha" they get is the source of the value in the question. In many cases they will have to synthesize the new thinking right on the spot. You can actually see it happening. Because of this, be aware of these dynamics:

- Wait for them to respond. Studies show that salespeople only wait about one second before either rephrasing their question, asking a new question, making an additional comment, or even trying to answer the question for the client. The urge to fill the silence is uncontrollable.

Higher level questions require that you give clients time to reflect and synthesize their answer. They will not answer in a single second. It is imperative that you wait at least three or four seconds before speaking, so that they can contemplate what you have asked them and formulate an answer.

Additionally, after their initial answer wait at least *another* three or four seconds because often the client is thinking out loud, and they will augment their answer shortly after their reply—but only if you stay quiet and allow them to finish their thoughts. In group situations it is very common for another person to jump in and add information or detail. You want this. Studies show that when we have patience at these two intervals, we get two to five times more information from buyers. More importantly, however, is that clients value their experience far greater.

It can take an amazing amount of self-control to pause during these two periods as clients cognate. Until you've practiced it, the urge to jump in can be uncontrollable, so here is a tip that will make this process easy: Take notes. Visibly show that you are preparing to take notes as you ask your question. As they respond begin writing their comments and you will automatically get the four seconds of silence you need to prompt more information. After their reply silently take notes again. Very often they will continue to provide more and more information during your silent note taking. It's quite remarkable.

- Because high-level questions require more thought on behalf of prospects, it is important that you use them judiciously. They require more mental "CPU cycles" than ordinary questions so be selective about what you ask. Your mileage will vary, but two or three questions at this level is probably ideal for any given encounter. My personal experience is that five high-value questions is likely the upper limit in a single encounter before they start to perceive your value-add questions negatively. Your delivery of these questions can make a lot of difference, but my advice is to aim for two or three and less than five.

In a future work I will deconstruct the craft of high-value questioning, but for now here are a few examples:

- As you assemble your evaluation team, how will you determine which priorities will be most heavily weighted?

- As you design what you feel will be the ideal solution, what criteria will you use to evaluate options?

- As you reflect on possible trade-offs or compromises, how will you determine which elements will be the most important?

- During your evaluation, what are the steps you will be going through as a company?

- As you reflect on your progress thus far, what do you anticipate will be the biggest challenges to integrating this into your current environment?

Questions are considered by many experts to be your most valuable tool. The right questions are facilitative and help both you and the buyer uncover what they value most. The right questions will uncover the hierarchy of each individual's preferences along with their preferred outcomes. They also reveal personal agendas and the influence dynamics between the players involved in the decision.

In addition to adding value, the right questions will:

- Engage your clients

- Direct their attention to the topics that are most important for them to consider

- Facilitate new connections in their minds and help them synthesize new understanding

- Assist clients in discovering their own answers

- Facilitate learning through articulation

- Enhance memory

- Elicit feedback

- Clarify issues and eliminate assumptions

- Increase confidence

Because high-value questions require planning before each meeting they differentiate you from competitors in a very big way.

"High-value questions require planning before each meeting."

Most importantly, the right questions are perceived as valuable. They build rapport and trust, they establish you as a consultant, and they prove that you and the client are aligned in your interests. Repeating this experience with clients and prospects during each encounter trains them to see you as a trusted advisor which keeps you close to them during and after the sale.

For those interested in exploring this subject further I highly recommend Deb Calvert's book *DISCOVER Questions Get You Connected: for professional sellers.* I agree with her statement, "There is no easier and more affordable way to create genuine, personalized value for each and every buyer."

Help Clients Better Understand Their Needs

One outcome of using superior questions is that your clients come to better understand their own needs. When you assist them in better understanding and objectifying their needs (and as a result what the requirements will be to meet those needs) you are adding value.

Performing an excellent discovery with the prospect will facilitate mutual understanding of what it will take for them to succeed. Your discovery can also help them better understand their own internal dynamics and help them get a firm grasp of the tools needed to move their organization forward.

How to perform a professional discovery will be the subject of a future work. Suffice it to say that professional discovery skills on your part are essential for both you and your prospect's success. They will always value a professionally executed discovery.

Help Clients See the Path to Success

When clients are considering a new project, idea, or solution they will be unsure about how its adoption will actually effect their organization. The path to success is cloudy for them. When the steps ahead are unclear, they perceive heightened risk. That heightened risk very often causes them to slow down or even halt their progress as they assess all the dynamics associated with moving forward.

When you present a clear vision of how your prospect can achieve their objectives or help them develop their own vision, you are adding value.

With complex projects and objectives it is common that prospective clients are in completely new territory. They may embark on a project such as this only once in a lifetime. In that sense, you are in a perfect position to add value precisely because you are frequently involved in such projects. Your experiences represent tremendous value, so share them— tips, stories, planning tools, sample project plans, outcomes of similar clients, etc. Help them see that there is a clear set of steps and actions that they can take that will guarantee success.

"When you present a clear vision of how your prospect can achieve their objectives or help them develop their own vision, you are adding value."

In some cases, the value you bring in these areas can surpass the value of the solution itself and will position you as a consultant and trusted advisor. Be sure to leverage this *unexpected value* in every opportunity.

Share New Ideas

New ideas represent a limitless area of value. Ron Baker, founder of VeraSage Institute and author of *Mind Over Matter,* says, "Ideas have always and everywhere been more valuable than the physical act of carrying them out. In the arena of business, ideas have an enormous capacity to apply knowledge to knowledge, thereby increasing innovation and wealth."

To be sure, not every idea you bring will be weighed equally from your prospect's perspective. Some ideas will be valued more heavily than others. However, there is value inherent in the ideas you bring regardless of whether or not your prospect employs them. Ideally they will see great benefit from the ideas you bring, but it's not necessary that they use the idea for them to perceive its value. So offer them all the valuable ideas that you can.

Your experiences in implementing your products and services will likely far outweigh your prospect's experience. So most of your thoughts and ideas in this area will be seen as helpful. Share how your other clients have:

- Reduced costs

- Increased revenues

- Garnered additional business

- Saved time

- Managed resources

- Improved a process

- Improved quality/outcomes

- Simplified tasks

- Solved a particular problem/challenge

- Successfully implemented something

- Made their job easier

- Used their existing solution in a new way

- Utilized a service that they had overlooked

I like to think of this area of ideas as "best practices" for your clients. The potential in delivering valuable ideas is virtually immeasurable, so take time to identify what your prospects would find most valuable and build on it. These can be delivered informally and conversationally or compiled into white papers and other useful reports. Tailor them to your prospect's situation to maximize their perception of value.

James Muir

Deliver Education

Delivering insight is really about education. If you become a diligent student of best practices in your industry and educate your clients and prospects every time you encounter them, they will value and anticipate every interaction with you. They will be eager to share their new resource (you) with others and that will help you develop new relationships and opportunities.

Consider developing educational sessions either occasionally or on a regular basis. The cost is usually minimal, yet (just as with the other items listed above) the perception of value the customer receives can be huge.

When possible, collect feedback from attendees regarding the value they've receive as a result of these educational efforts and use these examples as valuable adjuncts to share in future educational sessions.

Share News, Trigger Events, and Insights from Their Industry

Sharing news, trigger events, and insights from their industry can add value to your meetings so long as your prospects are not already aware of the information. The key, as we previously outlined, is that it must be new and unexpected. By and large, sharing industry news and events falls more towards the weaker end of the spectrum when it comes to adding value to your encounters, but if it's actually news to them and relevant, it will be seen as valuable.

"In some cases, the value you bring in these areas can surpass the value of the solution itself and will position you as a consultant and trusted advisor."

Become a Domain Expert

In order to consistently provide insight, innovative thinking, and unanticipated solutions put forth the effort to become a top expert in your domain. Where your expertise and facilitation intersect, your clients will find great value and, you will find great success.

Additional Resources

If you would like to further explore how to add value to your sales encounters go to PureMuir.com to find more creative ideas on this topic.

Closing Secret #13 - The key to adding value is preparation.

Conclusion

By consistently delivering value on each and every encounter we train our prospects and clients to see us as valuable resources, domain experts, and trusted advisors who can help them achieve the outcomes they desire.

How we sell is a sample of how we solve, and prospects are sampling our value on each and every encounter. They sum up their experiences with us and extrapolate them into what they think their future experiences will be with both us and the companies we represent. This is an extremely strong sales dynamic that can work for you or against you on every interaction.

It is critical that we consistently deliver *Unexpected Value* on each and every sales encounter. Fortunately, the number of ways to add value to any given sales encounter is virtually limitless. The key is to prepare. Professionals do not "wing it."

It starts with thoughtful preparation. We've already thought through the first two Magic Pre-call Questions:

1.   Why should this client see me?

2.   What do I want the client to do?

It is the third question, "How can I provide value on this encounter?" that is almost universally ignored in selling today.

Very few salespeople give any thought to the value prospects will receive from meeting with you. If you aren't able to articulate what the prospect will gain from your meeting, you can safely assume that the meeting will be a waste of time (not the kind of sample we want to deliver).

Each sales encounter must be inherently valuable.

By thoughtfully preparing in advance, we can share something that this specific prospect will find valuable at this specific time, every single time we meet. Our clients and prospects will find each meeting with us both valuable and enjoyable, and they will look forward to continuing that pattern throughout the sales process and long after the sale is closed.

In the next chapter we will learn how to plan each encounter so that it is both maximally valuable and productive.

CHAPTER 10

Planning Your Next Encounter

"Planning maximizes the value of the call to the customer."

–David Brock

Congratulations! You are now fully equipped to plan and execute a high-value meeting with your prospective client. Being a professional means planning. Productivity and success doesn't happen by accident. It is the result of planning, commitment, and focused effort.

When you get right down to it, there are two strategic types of benefits to planning—tactical and contemplative.

Tactical - Planning is beneficial from a tactical perspective because it results in the actual words you will say, questions you will ask, and areas you will address. Knowing these in advance will greatly improve your confidence and your effectiveness. It will also produce an agenda (see below) which will give you and your prospect a clear awareness of where you are during the course of your meeting and the sequence you will follow.

Contemplative - Planning is beneficial from a contemplative perspective because it forces us to slow down and think in ways we wouldn't have otherwise. It allows us to contemplate what we don't know and reminds us to consider important dynamics that could be overlooked.

As sales professionals we tend to be action-oriented. We favor jumping right in to make something happen. For many, planning is unfamiliar or even uncomfortable territory. One of the marks of a true professional is working smart in addition to working hard.

In this chapter we will make planning quick and efficient for you by distilling all you have learned thus far into a set of easy-to-follow steps. First, let's review...

The 7 Primary Reasons to Plan Every Sales Encounter:

1. **You will be far more effective** - We learned earlier in the book that sales planning is strongly correlated with success. [1-3] Neil Rackham declared that their research findings at Huthwaite indicated that "Good selling depends on good planning more than any other single factor."[4]

2. **It increases the probability you will achieve your intended outcome** - The old expression "Failing to plan is planning to fail" is still true today. Knowing in advance what you want to achieve significantly increases your odds of achieving it.

3. **It will help you plan and remember the questions you want to ask** - Strong value-add questions are hard to create on the fly. Planning in advance will allow you to craft excellent questions and remind you to ask them in the heat of the moment.

4. **It creates a checklist of steps for you to follow** - Planning gives you a roadmap to gaining the contacts, information, and commitments you need for a successful outcome.

5. **It gives you time to prepare your Unexpected Value** - Considering what *unexpected value* is best for your prospective

client during your upcoming encounter depends on where your prospect is in their buying cycle. Planning ahead gives you the time to maximize your value.

6. **It increases the probability you will achieve your prospect's intended outcome** - You only succeed when your prospect or client succeeds. Consistently planning ahead ensures they will achieve what they expect—from this meeting as well as the entire sale.

7. **It differentiates you from the competition** - Few salespeople give much thought to planning their sales encounters in terms of the value their prospect will receive, so planning a cohesive and valuable meeting alone will differentiate you from your competition.

Closing Secret #14 - Productivity and success don't happen by accident. You and your meetings will be more productive when you plan.

In previous chapters we:

- Got our mindset right

- Defined our sales objective

- Defined our call objective

- Reviewed our value proposition

- Brainstormed our possible advances, and

- Created ways to provide unexpected value

If you have participated in all of the previous chapters and completed the exercises, planning your sales encounter will be very straightforward. At the end of this chapter, you'll find forms to help with this process, but the process itself does not require one. In fact it doesn't require any special tools beyond a simple piece of paper and a pen. It is also compatible and complementary with today's major sales methodologies. So if you are already using a sales methodology this will dovetail nicely into your current process.

The Six Elements of Sales Encounter Planning

Regardless of the methodology or tools you use to plan each sales encounter, you should cover these six elements:

1. Research

2. Value Proposition

3. Questions

4. Advances

5. Unexpected Value

6. Agenda

Research

The process of gathering, analyzing, and interpreting information about your prospect—their drivers and characteristics, market and sub-markets, challenges and financial status, goals and objectives, the particulars about this potential opportunity including other alternatives or solutions they may be considering—is the homework you do before your meeting.

As you research, consider:

- In what industry, market, and sub-market is your prospective client?

- What types of clients do they have?

- What are the drivers in their industry right now?

- What is their financial status?

- What are their goals and objectives?

Consider their current situation:

- What are the challenges regarding their current situation?

- What is the impact of their current situation and challenges?

- What hidden challenges might they encounter?

- What might the impact of those hidden challenges be?

- What risks are likely to be of greatest concern to them?

- What fears might they be feeling about a making a bad decision?

Consider the importance of each specific issue:

- What are the specific issues this client is facing?

- How great is the impact of each specific issue?

- What is their priority for resolving each specific issue?

Consider their decision-making process:

- Who will be involved in the decision-making process?

- What process will they go through as they evaluate?

- Where are they in the process now?

- What have they accomplished up to this point?

- What is the scheduled time for a decision to be made?

- What are the drivers behind the timing of their decision?

- What criteria will they use to determine their ultimate solution?

- How will they go about making their final decision?

- What other solutions or alternatives are they or might they be considering?

- What are the pros and cons of those possible solutions?

Consider the resources and constraints they may facing:

- Who on their team will be involved in implementing the project?

- What thought has been given to a budget for the results they are seeking?

- What has kept them from solving this problem already?

- What other improvement opportunities might they have overlooked?

Then, consider any additional research you might need to conduct before your meeting.

Value Proposition

This is the answer to "Why should this prospect see me?" It describes what about your offer is of benefit to your prospective client. It is the measurable value you bring. If you have not met with your prospect before, then you will have a *value hypothesis* or best guess as to what will benefit them. Your value proposition is the primary factor that determines how you are positioned with this prospect. At the minimum your value proposition will have a metric (a measurable performance indicator), a direction (does it increase it or lower it), and magnitude (how much it affects the metric).

Things to consider for your value proposition:

- Why should this prospect see me now? What is my value hypothesis?

- What tangible value can I bring to this client?

- What are the metrics that measure the value I bring?

- What is the magnitude of the value I bring?

- What evidence do I have that I can help?

Questions

The information gathering and value-adding questions you intend to ask your prospective client should be developed prior to your encounter. True value-adding questions are those to which the client does not already know the answer. They require thought, encourage reflection, and advance the conversation into new territory. When we prompt our prospect's higher-level thinking we are literally adding value. Asking tough, powerful questions define you as a consultant and communicate that you have a genuine intent to help. You should prepare two or three high-value questions for every encounter.

Consider the following when developing questions:

- What additional information do I need that has not been answered by my research?

- What information questions do I intend to ask the client?

- What is the priority of each question? If I'm not able to ask all of my questions, which should I ask first?

- What value-add questions do I intend to ask?

- What questions can I ask that will stimulate and facilitate my prospect's understanding?

Advances

Your planned advances answer, "What do I want my prospect to do as a result of this meeting?" It is the action(s) you want them to take. An *ideal advance* is the highest level of commitment you can reasonably expect them to make as a result of this encounter. Advances should be specific and measurable, center on the action the prospect will take, move the sale forward, and be reasonable from their perspective. You should plan an ideal advance as well as several alternate advances in the event that your ideal proves unrealistic.

Consider first, your ideal advance:

- What is my primary call objective?

- Is my primary call objective specific and measureable? Does it center on the action the client will take; move the sale forward; reasonable from the buyer's perspective?

- What is the perfect close phrase (which you are about to learn) I will use to obtain this advance?

Consider alternate/additional advances if you are unable to achieve your ideal advance, or if the meeting is going extremely well:

- What are my secondary/backup objectives for this meeting?

- What alternate or additional advances could I request as a result of this meeting?

- What is the perfect close phrase I will use for each of these?

Consider the minimum advance you are willing to settle for:

- What is the smallest advance I am willing to accept and still move forward?

- What is the perfect close phrase I will use to obtain this advance?

Unexpected Value

This is the unanticipated value your prospect receives as a result of your meeting and should be delivered on each and every sales encounter. Delivering insight is the primary way you add value. There are nearly infinite ways to do this. Those might include: Asking powerful questions; facilitating understanding; helping clients see the path to success; sharing new ideas and tips; delivering education; sharing news, trigger events and insights about their industry.

Ask yourself, "What unexpected value will I bring to this meeting?"

Agenda

This is the list of items to be discussed during your meeting. The prospect's stated interests should be the main focus. Confirm your agenda with them and make sure it meets their expectation of what they want covered. You should have an agenda for every encounter. You will learn more about what makes an effective agenda in the following chapter.

For your agenda, consider the purpose of the meeting:

- What is the meeting's primary purpose from my prospect's perspective?

- What specific directives or expectations does my prospect have for this meeting?

Consider those in attendance:

- Who from my team will join me?

- Who from my prospect's organization will (or should be) in attendance?

- What are their names and titles?

- What will be each participant's objectives?

Consider your initial comments and interactions:

- What will your opening comment be?

- What will you state as the purpose of your meeting?

- What new introductions are needed (either on the prospect's team or your own)?

- How will you summarize your understanding of the prospect's current situation and challenges?

Consider your positioning:

- What strengths do I bring to this opportunity?

- What might the prospective client consider to be my vulnerabilities?

- What can I do or say to increase my credibility with them?

Consider the physical logistics:

- What is the proposed date, time, and estimated length?

- Where will the meeting take place and in what format?

- Who on the client's side is coordinating the meeting?

- Have all of the details of the meeting been confirmed?

- Have all the materials needed for the meeting been confirmed?

- Have attendee schedules been checked?

- What time do you need to begin wrapping up?

Example Forms

Use the following forms to walk yourself through the process. You can also find downloadable forms at PureMuir.com.

Research Planning Form

METRICS

What metrics does the client use to measure their objective results? What are these results now? What do they want them to be? What is the value of the difference? What is the value over time?

Metric	Current Value	Desired Value	Value of Difference	Value Over Time

DECISION MAKING PROCESS

Who will be involved in the decision making process?

What process will they go through as they evaluate? Where are they at in that process now? What have they done to this point?

What is the time frame for a decision to be made? What are the drivers?

What criteria will they use to determine the ultimate solution? How will they make a decision?

What other solutions/alternatives are they or might they be considering?

OPTIONS/RESOURCES/CONSTRAINTS

What other improvement opportunities may the client be unaware of?

Who on their team will be involved in implementing the project?

Has the client given any thought to a budget for the results they are seeking?

What has kept the client from solving this problem already?

2

VALUE PROPOSITION / VALUE HYPOTHESIS

Why should this client see me now? What is my value hypothesis?

What tangible value can I bring to this client?

What are the metrics that measure the value I can bring?

What is the magnitude of the value I can bring?

What evidence do I have that I can help?

POSITIONING

What strengths do I bring to this opportunity?

What might the client consider to be my vulnerabilities?

QUESTIONS

	Priority
Information Questions: What additional information do I need?	
Value-Add Questions: What questions can I ask that will stimulate and facilitate my client's understanding?	

ADDITIONAL RESEARCH

What additional research do I need to conduct before my meeting?

SALES OBJECTIVE

What is my sales objective for this opportunity? (*Sales objectives should: 1. Be for a specific product/service, 2. Be Measureable (i.e. quantity), 3. Have a target date for completion, 4. Be realistic from client's perspective.*)

BRING UNEXPECTED VALUE

What unexpected value can I bring to this meeting?

Sales Encounter Planning Form

Once your research is complete you will be better able to plan your sales encounter. Your awareness of gaps in your research and additional information that you need will help formulate the questions you will ask. Remember though, the meeting is not all about you. It is important that you make the meeting inherently valuable for your client. To that end you need to draw on your research to plan the sales encounter itself.

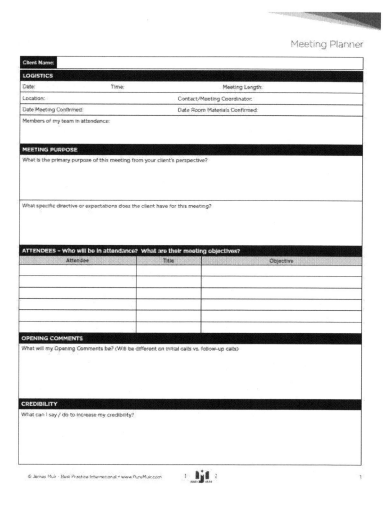

Meeting Planner

NEW INTRODUCTIONS

What new introductions are needed? (either on the client's team or your team)

SUMMARY OF YOUR UNDERSTANDING

What is your summation of the client's current situation and challenges?

State the purpose of the current meeting:

What has changed since the last time you spoke?

Confirm timeframe if previously established. Are you still shooting for date xx/xx/xxxx?

QUESTIONS

	Priority
Information Questions: What additional information do I need?	
Value-Add Questions: What questions can I ask that will stimulate and facilitate my client's understanding?	

ISSUES/CHALLENGES

	Impact	Priority
What are the client's issues/challenges? Have their priorities changed?		

METRICS

What metrics does the client use to measure their objective results? What are these results now? What do they want them to be? What is the value of the difference? What is the value over time?

Metric	Current Value	Desired Value	Value of Difference	Value Over Time

VALUE PROPOSITION / VALUE HYPOTHESIS

Why should this client see me now? What is my value hypothesis?

What tangible value can I bring to this client?

What are the metrics that measure the value I can bring?

What is the magnitude of the value I can bring?

What evidence do I have that I can help?

POSITIONING

What strengths do I bring to this opportunity?

What might the client consider to be my vulnerabilities?

  3

CALL OBJECTIVES / ADVANCES

What is my primary call objective? *(Call Objectives should be: 1. Specific & measurable, 2. Center on the action the client will take, 3. Move the sale forward, 4. Be reasonable from the client's perspective)*

What is my ideal Advance for this meeting?

Perfect Close phrase:

SECONDARY / BACKUP OBJECTIVES

What are my secondary/backup objectives?

-
-
-

What are my alternate/additional Advances for this meeting?

-
-
-

Perfect Close phrases:

-
-
-

MINIMUM ADVANCE

What is the smallest advance I am willing to accept and still move forward?

Perfect Close phrase:

BRING UNEXPECTED VALUE

What unexpected value can I bring to this meeting?

> *"The meeting is not about you. Make the meeting inherently valuable for your client."*

Conclusion

Using a planning process will greatly improve the effectiveness of your meetings. More effective meetings will solidify your credibility, perceived authority, and differentiate you from your competition. More effective meetings mean your clients will be more likely to achieve their desired solutions while you enjoy higher close ratios, more closed opportunities, and greater personal success.

Follow this straightforward checklist of planning steps, and you will be able to repeat your success over and over again.

Next up we will discover how to create an effective agenda that will maximize the value and impact of each meeting.

CHAPTER 11

Creating a Collaborative Meeting Agenda

"The secret of your success is determined by your daily agenda."

–John C. Maxwell

It would be easy to forgo creating a meeting agenda and just wing it, but that would be a big mistake. Agendas are far more powerful than most people realize. They represent a valuable tool that mitigates risk and greatly improves the likelihood that each meeting will have the outcome you desire.

Agendas provide nine important functions:

1. Position you as a true professional and advisor

2. Heighten the importance to your meeting

3. Define the meeting's objectives

4. Show potential attendees why it is important to attend

5. Set expectations

6. Help invitees prepare

7. Provide structure and sequence to the meeting

8. Dedicate time to establish action items and next steps

9. Provide a way to measure the success of the meeting

A solid meeting agenda ensures that the time invested in it has a valuable return for everyone involved. Your goals are to obtain your ideal advance and deliver your prospect both edification and unexpected value. The best way achieve this win-win dynamic is to collaborate with your client on the agenda.

Collaborating with your client or prospect on the meeting agenda achieves a three-fold purpose:

1. It ensures you don't overlook any key objectives.

2. It ensures the depth and duration of each item stays within the meeting's overall timeframe.

3. It increases buy-in from attendees who have a hand in designing the meeting.

By asking for input from your prospect along with their key staff members, departments, and managers who should be involved, the likelihood of your success increases dramatically. Their input, combined with yours, regarding topics to include and how much time should be devoted to each will garner greater attendance, acceptance, and support for your meeting.

In complex sales where many parties may be involved, start the process well in advance as requesting the input of many people can take a considerable amount of time. The more people involved, the longer the process can take. Do not wait until the last minute to formulate a collaborative agenda. A very straightforward agenda can take a week to complete simply due to the number of parties involved. So, as soon as you're aware that a meeting is needed, begin the process of formulating an agenda with your prospect.

If the prospect is actively adding agenda items, that is a good thing. They are openly sharing. Let them continue to share. Sometimes this process can result in far too many agenda items to cover in the allotted time. That's a good sign of engagement but you will need to digest all that they have shared and narrow the focus to a meeting that is manageable. Acknowledge the importance of the non-included items and set up another time to cover these in another discussion.

As you revise the agenda, share updates and changes with your key contact and any other people involved to ensure the agenda still makes sense.

Now, let's review the functions of your meeting agenda.

Agendas Position You as a True Professional and Advisor

Your agenda is a reflection of you, your company, and your professionalism. Clients and prospects alike will project much about the value of the meeting and your professionalism from the quality of your agenda. Make sure your agenda reflects the professional image you want by also looking professional in its appearance.

It is helpful to maintain a meeting agenda template to get you started. Your whole agenda should fit on a single piece of paper. Simplicity is key. It should be clear and easy to follow at a glance.

You can find several example agenda templates to aid you at PureMuir. com.

> *"Clients and prospects alike will project much about the value of the meeting and your professionalism from the quality of your agenda."*

If you have attachments for the agenda (e.g., reports, documents, images, etc.), include them in your email and consider putting them online via secure hyperlink so attendees can access these reference documents. If they are not needed prior to the meeting, consider distributing a hard copy at the meeting.

Agendas Add Importance to Your Meeting

All by themselves, simply because they exist, agendas will increase your prospects' perceived importance of your meetings. One of my C-level executive friends uses the existence of a written agenda to determine whether or not he will attend any given meeting. He told me, "If it's not important enough to have a written agenda, it's not important enough for me to attend." Your written agenda will enhance your professional image and your prospect's perception that you are able to effectively make things happen.

Agendas Define the Objective(s) of the Meeting

The meeting objective drives everything else. It shows each attendee why it's important to attend, sets expectations as to what the meeting will accomplish, helps prospects prepare, and provides a way to determine the meeting's effectiveness. If you're not sure why you are meeting, chances are your stakeholders won't know either.

By clearly outlining meeting objectives you are far more likely to get the attendance you need, and more importantly, the acceptance you need for your change initiative. If you haven't already, you should identify all stakeholders that will be involved in your meeting and consider what their personal objectives might be. Remember that companies don't buy things—people do. Each of the individual stakeholders will have their own objectives which may or may not be in alignment with the other members of the group. Understanding each stakeholder's personal objectives will greatly improve your stated meeting objective.

Phrasing your stated meeting objective - As previously mentioned, it is paramount that prospects anticipate that our meeting with them is going to be valuable. So, the primary focus should be the prospect's agenda—their stated interests, challenges, goals, etc.—not yours. Although we have our own objectives for the meeting, the meeting objective should be stated from the prospect's perspective and focused on the outcomes they hope to achieve. There should be no mention of products and services whatsoever, only the outcomes they hope to achieve by utilizing those things.

To the degree possible, your stated meeting objective should be broad enough to interest all relevant parties in the meeting. The narrower your audience, the easier this becomes. For example, if your attendees are 100% IT staff then your stated meeting objective can be narrowed to describe technical issues of interest. However, when your audience includes people from executive management, finance, IT, operations, the legal department, and field personnel it can become more challenging. When this happens zoom out and consider the outcomes that are important to everyone when phrasing your meeting objective.

To sum up, your stated meeting objective should:

1. Be stated from the prospect's perspective.

2. Focus on the outcomes they hope to achieve.

3. Be broad enough to be of interest to all attendees.

Examples of stated meeting objectives:

- Explore best practices for growing business despite challenges with lower customer engagement.

- Review & discuss implications & trade-off of 100% cloud deployment.

- Discuss strategies for preparing for value-based reimbursement.

- Review practical steps for reducing risk & simplifying regulatory compliance issues.

- Scrutinize the implications of upgrading solutions & how to successfully implement organizational change.

- Review & discuss strategies for preparing for reimbursement models that place a greater share of financial risk on the organization.

- Examine the top 5 strategies for reducing operational costs while maintaining quality.

- Discuss the current options for reducing claim denial losses in the context of regulatory change.

- Evaluate the financial & operational implications of recent regulation & how to best address them.

- Analyze strategies for reducing executive & employee workload while improving quality.

- Evaluate technical specifications & tradeoffs of deployment models.

- Determine & decide which approach is best for [ABC Co.].

- Discuss & finalize agreement terms & conditions.

You'll find that the first word in each of these examples is a verb. I'll admit my favorite word to use is "Discuss" because it implies the kind of collaboration I tend to look for in my meetings. Here are some other words you will find useful for phrasing your stated meeting objective:

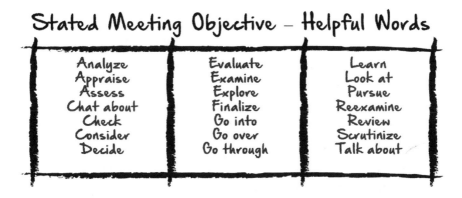

Stated Meeting Objective – Helpful Words

Analyze	Evaluate	Learn
Appraise	Examine	Look at
Assess	Explore	Pursue
Chat about	Finalize	Reexamine
Check	Go into	Review
Consider	Go over	Scrutinize
Decide	Go through	Talk about

Stated meeting objectives help you plan - Another benefit of phrasing your stated meeting objective from the prospect's perspective is it helps you plan the meeting in a way that adds value for them. The more concrete your meeting objectives, the more focused your agenda will be. It also suggests what questions and issues may arise and will help you be more prepared for these discussions when they happen.

Agendas Show Potential Attendees Why They Should Attend

The worst thing that can happen to your meeting is having little or no attendance. No progress can be made if the right people do not attend your meeting. Meeting value, like beauty, is in the eye of the beholder. Until we articulate the value of the meeting in our agenda, potential attendees will assume that your meeting will be the typical waste of time that most corporate meetings are.

By outlining the purpose of the meeting, topics to be discussed, and its time frame, potential attendees can easily determine whether or not they should attend. The best way to do this is to explicitly state what the outcome objective is. When we tie the outcome to important objectives the prospect wants to achieve, attendees will make space on their calendar for your meeting—which is tremendously beneficial because you will have the right people in the room to help your initiative succeed. This alone can shorten your sales cycle. Having key individuals attend or not attend can make and break sales. Your agenda shows them why they need to attend and prepares you to satisfy their expectations.

Having the right parties in attendance also provides a measure of risk control after the sale is complete. Stakeholders who participated in the evaluation stages are more likely to feel their concerns were listened to, that they influenced the decision, and that their needs were addressed. This higher level of communication and participation reduces possible negative reactions to future, unforeseen incidents.

If your solution requires dramatic change for your prospect, sending your agenda in advance familiarizes stakeholders with the initiative prior to your meeting and eliminates possible surprise responses that occur when they learn of these things for the first time during your meeting.

Agendas Set the Client's Expectations

Have you ever attended a meeting where a party's interests was not addressed and it created problems? I have seen firsthand, domineering stakeholders completely derail meetings by repeatedly inserting their personal agenda. This can be especially challenging when the domineering party is a high-ranking official.

When you collaborate on the agenda in advance, everyone's expectations regarding the meeting's purpose and the topics to be addressed are clearly spelled out. It doesn't guarantee that someone won't try and hijack your meeting (though it does reduce the chances), but it does give you the ability to say something like, "Those are all good points. The purpose of this meeting is to X. We plan to cover that topic in an upcoming meeting." I have used this many times to reel-in high ranking officials who were not adequately briefed on the purpose of the meeting, and it works very well.

Meeting Agendas Help Your Invitees Prepare

Knowing the purpose and the outline of topics gives attendees a clear understanding of what to prepare for the meeting. Some meetings require specific information and will reach an impasse without that information. Agendas eliminate excuses that participants aren't ready to discuss a subject because they didn't know it was going to be brought up. You can go as far as to include an "Information Required" section of your agenda so your invitees will clearly see what is needed in order to have a productive meeting.

Be sure to communicate any facts or figures that will be necessary for a productive discussion. If appropriate, you may consider (with the assistance of your prospect) specifically assigning the person responsible for providing the information. When specific individuals are made responsible for their participation, the meeting will take on new significance for those participants.

Of course, agendas also prepare you. Your level of preparedness will directly translate to the meeting's degree of success.

Agendas Provide the Meeting's Structure and Sequence

Agendas identify the specific topics open for discussion and prevent others from adding new issues to the meeting. Agendas also eliminate the guesswork as to whether or not a particular issue will be discussed.

Agendas keep everyone focused in ways that simple verbal guidance cannot. Essentially, it's a written roadmap that guides participants through what needs to be accomplished and encourages them to stay on track while driving the conversation toward conclusion.

Your agenda should be specific enough to elicit adequate preparation and intelligent discussion. If your agenda is too broad, attendees may not be prepared to adequately drill into the subject matter.

The meeting's content must be relevant to the interests of all participants, and within their framework of understanding. If any agenda items are too technical in nature for certain participants, you will lose their attention. Conversely, if content is overly simplistic, attendees may resort to texting or checking email during your meeting.

There is no one-size-fits-all meeting agenda. While templates can give us a jump start in creating our meeting agenda, each agenda should be tailored to the specific objectives of your meeting. To jumpstart your process, download several agenda templates at PureMuir.com.

The structure of every agenda should contain the following elements, though the exact elements and wording of your agenda should be tailored from meeting to meeting:

1. **Logistics** - The date, start and end time, and the location of your meeting. It should include a title as well as a list of invited attendees.

2. **Meeting Objectives** - State the objective purpose of the meeting in a single sentence, if possible. As outlined above, make sure it is: a. Stated from the client's perspective; b. Focused on the outcomes they hope to achieve; c. Broad enough to be of interest to all attendees. State a specific desired outcome (a decision or action item), if possible.

3. **Housekeeping** - This includes welcomes and introductions as well as accommodations regarding food, bathrooms, parking validation, etc. You may also choose to do an agenda overview before jumping into the first item.

4. **Items** - Agenda items are the "meat" of your agenda. They help to communicate why your attendees are there and serve to keep your meeting on track. They are the topics you plan to discuss in the appropriate sequence.

    The sequence, or order, can make a big difference in how your meeting flows. By sequencing agenda items you are, in effect, prioritizing them. This will give you the freedom to address things in the correct order, and maintaining that order, since someone anxious to cover a particular item can see that it is coming up. If your meeting calls for a particular party to lead an item of discussion, note this on the agenda, so they can anticipate the preparation and timing involved.

    The sequence gives attendees a mental feel for where you are in the meeting and delivers a feeling of progress as you step

James Muir

through each item. It is a good idea to front-load the meeting with the highest priority topics. In doing so, if the meeting is cut short without covering the entire agenda you can rest assured that the most critical items have been addressed and that less important items can wait for a follow-up meeting.

Similarly, with the mutually agreed-upon agenda as your guide, you are able to effectively control the meeting and ensure that the group does not get bogged down in any one area. When you see this phenomenon coming, you can "parking lot" the topic and continue moving forward in the name of sticking to the agenda and keeping the meeting on schedule.

A timed agenda can be especially helpful since a ticking clock is motivating, and you can move on to the next item when the allotted time is up. If you have concerns that time may get away from you, include a written time frame for each item. Even if you don't put this in writing, you should estimate how much time you will likely need for each topic so you're able to keep your meeting on schedule.

However, just because you have outlined the general sequence of the meeting, it doesn't mean you can't be flexible. To the contrary, having a structure for the meeting will greatly simplify your ability to navigate and maneuver accordingly.

It is important to be both disciplined and flexible at the same time. Have a plan (that possibly includes timings) to address each segment of your meeting. Approach your meeting with the intent to adhere to those timings, but if the conversation is highly beneficial, don't be afraid to let it run long. Likewise, if the conversation is dragging or rehashing, use the agenda productively to move on.

— 172 —

The framework of the agenda gives you the Zen-like ability to flexibly expand or contract as well as stay on or move outside the agenda in whatever way makes the meeting most valuable for everyone involved.

5. **Next Steps/Action Items** - This is the opportunity at the end of your meeting to determine the action items and next steps necessary to keep the project rolling forward. Have your ideal advance and secondary/backup advances planned. This is when you will use your pre-planned Perfect Close phrase (which you are about to learn). Discuss all action items and next steps. For each item determine:

   a. What needs to be done

   b. To whom it is assigned

   c. The target timeframe to complete it

This is also the time to schedule the next meeting date with the client.

In addition to these items, you may also consider including an "outcome agenda" in which you briefly note the outcome being sought for the topic or subtopic. This can be amazingly effective, especially when subsequent agenda items require decisions or consensus on previous agenda items.

Remember to weave your own call objective and unexpected value into the agenda. In most cases prospects are not open to receiving unexpected value until their main issues have been addressed, so it is generally best to include that value toward the middle or end of your agenda. Be careful not to telegraph your unexpected value in a way that reveals it, or even worse turns it into an expectation. It should be just what it's called—*unexpected value*.

The meeting is a win-win when both you and your prospect have met your objectives.

Agendas Provide Time to Establish Action Items and Next steps

In order for you to facilitate and affect positive change for your prospects and keep their project moving forward, it is vital that you allow adequate time toward the end of your agenda (as outlined above) to establish action items and next steps.

Business meetings are infamous for being unproductive and a waste of time. The number-one complaint about most meetings is "nothing was accomplished." Don't let your meeting become another casualty in the pile of dead meetings at the corporate assembly graveyard. Make sure something *does* get accomplished in each and every interaction by allocating time to establish next steps and action items. When the meeting arrives at this item, thank the participants for the valuable discussion and transition to Next Steps.

Address any obvious action items that have arisen during the course of the meeting and work through any the next steps. Be careful to define:

- What needs to be done

- To whom it is assigned (you or the prospect and which person specifically owns it)

- The target timeframe to complete it

Sometimes, sales reps have concerns about committing prospective clients to completion dates for action items or next steps. Relax. Simply ask something like, "When should I check back with you on X?" That will establish your target timeframe.

This section of the meeting is a good place for you to get commitment on your ideal advance as well as secondary or fall-back advances which, of course, you will have defined prior to even creating the agenda. So, after addressing the obvious action items, you will use The Perfect Close (which you will shortly learn) for your ideal advance. Regardless of their answer, follow up by suggesting one of your secondary or fall-back advances and repeat as needed. This will make more sense after the next chapter.

> *"It is vital that you allow time in your agenda to establish action items and next steps."*

This is, literally, the most important part of your meeting. Your prospects expect you to help them make the positive changes that will bring about their desired results. They expect you to encourage them to become better than they are. You will see in the next chapter how facilitative and non-confrontational this is. Push your clients and prospects toward improvement. Accept the challenge. Be their coach and guide them through each little commitment it takes to achieve their goals.

Understand, this is much more than you advancing your sale. This is leadership. So few people have true mentors and leaders in their life. So when you arrive on the scene with a path that leads them to improvement, and you guide them through it—however challenging or difficult it may be; however narrow in its scope—they will thank you.

> *"This is much more than you advancing your sale. This is leadership."*

This is also the time, while everyone is still present, to schedule the next meeting date. If the meeting disperses without setting the next date, it will make it that much harder to schedule the next meeting. Take advantage of everyone being in one place to get this settled. If your request is met with any uncertainty, then suggest to "pencil in a date" that can always be changed later. This ensures that you have something on the books and a commitment for further collaboration.

Always end every meeting with:

1. A review of the agreed-upon action items, and

2. The date for the next meeting

As a follow up, in an email to the attendees, thank them for the productive meeting, summarize what was discussed, list the action item assignments and deadlines, confirm the next meeting date, and begin the collaborative process of creating the next agenda. This is professional and ensures that everyone is on the same page.

> *"Always end every meeting with a review of the agreed upon action items and the date for the next meeting."*

Agendas Provide a Way to Measure the Success of Your Meeting

Because agendas include a stated meeting objective, they provide an excellent way for both you and your prospect to judge whether or not the meeting achieved its goal. From our client's perspective, we want them to walk out of the meeting thinking, "Man, that was a good meeting! I'm glad I attended."

Because you planned your meeting with an ideal advance as well as secondary/backup advances, it's simple to measure the success of your meeting. Were you able to accomplish your call objectives? Did the client achieve theirs? Why or why not? Is another meeting required? Setting call objectives allows you to continuously improve the effectiveness of your meetings.

Closing Secret #15 - Agendas are powerful tools that greatly improve the likelihood that each meeting will have the outcome you desire.

Conclusion

It is unprofessional to not have a meeting agenda. Not having an agenda sends the message that you are a time-waster, not a value creator. Non-professionals dismiss creating an agenda and just wing it. That is a big mistake because agendas are far more powerful than most people realize.

A well crafted agenda will have a strong effect on the outcome of the meeting and it can exert influence before the meeting even happens. Agendas are valuable tools that greatly improve the likelihood that your meetings will have the outcomes you desire.

Meeting agendas produce a tremendous return for a modest investment of time and greatly improve effectiveness.

One of the biggest benefits of meeting agendas is that they provide a logical and natural way to advance the sale. This is the time to help them advance toward their goals. Show them the way. Show them each commitment is a step in the right direction. Encourage and challenge them to take action. When they have accomplished their objective they will be grateful, thankful, and will credit you as a contributor to their success. This is the sweet spot of selling.

James Muir

CHAPTER 12

The Perfect Close

*"If the language you use to close makes you uncomfortable,
then it probably isn't good closing language."*

- Anthony Iannarino

I f you jumped right to this chapter to discover how The Perfect Close works, you are in for a treat. The approach can be learned in five minutes. However, I encourage you to utilize the other chapters of this book to help you maximize your approach to The Perfect Close and ultimately every client encounter. You will benefit greatly by combining The Perfect Close with the preliminary work set forth in previous chapters. In doing so you will shorten your sales cycle, maximize the impact of each meeting, and advance your sale in a way that differentiates you from your competition.

In an ideal world we would all be masters at selling, and we would all have a perfect understanding of where the client is in their buying process, and we would only ask a direct closing question at exactly the right moment. Yes, that would be ideal.

But the truth is, we are all on the road to mastery, and we are all in different places along that road. Do we have to achieve mastery before we can ask a closing question? Why train and debate when the right time is to ask a closing question when we can just craft an approach that *doesn't require mastery* and can be asked at virtually any time without risk?

This is one of the key things that make The Perfect Close perfect. New and inexperienced professionals can learn and use it successfully right out of the chute. They can become productive with the technique almost immediately. And ironically, there is no reason to change it as one's experience improves. I have been selling for several decades now, and I still use The Perfect Close almost daily.

The Perfect Close is simple. You only need to learn two questions. Even better, in many cases you will only need to use *one* of those two questions.

The Perfect Close Questions

There is an initial question and a follow-up question in The Perfect Close. In addition to learning how to apply these two questions, it is helpful for you to know some logical advances for your prospective client. It's not required, but it helps.

Here are the questions:

Initial Question: "Does it make sense for us to X?"

Follow-Up Question: "What is a good next step?"

Simple, huh? Let's examine question one.

"Question one of the perfect close is: "Does it makes sense for us to X?"

The formula is: "Does it makes sense for us to X?"

In this case the "X" is a logical advance for your sale.

Here are some examples:

- "Does it make sense to talk about scheduling a site visit for you so you can see the product in a live environment?"

- "Does it make sense for us to talk about putting together a financial assessment of your current situation?"

- "Does it make sense for us to talk about getting your credit approved while we go through the other details together?"

- "Does it make sense for us to talk about putting together some samples so you can try them out?"

- "Does it make sense for us to schedule some time with our creative department to give you some ideas on what your options might be?"

- "Does it make sense for us to talk about doing a workflow analysis so we can see where the best efficiencies can be gained?"

- "Does it make sense for us to put together a statement of work for you so we can start getting an idea the project's scope?"

- "Does it make sense for us to schedule an appraiser to check out the property so we can get an idea of its market value?"

- "Does it make sense for us to schedule a physical for you so we can see what kind of rates we can get?"

- "Does it make sense for us to put together a proposal for you so we can start sizing up the investment?"

- "Does it make sense for us to schedule a meeting with your team so we can get their input on what would be most beneficial for them?"

- "Does it make sense for us to schedule some time with our technical team so we can get a clearer picture of the requirements?"

- "Does it make sense for me to meet your executive sponsor so we can get some specifics about her objectives for the project?"

- "Does it make sense for us to schedule a demonstration so your whole team can see it in action?"

- "Does it make sense for us to talk about wrapping everything up?"

The Nuances of Question One

The stem of question one, "Does it make sense…," is so simple that it's easy to miss its sublime power. Experience has also taught me that for those new to the technique it is easy to misinterpret what the question is really asking and get it wrong. So with that in mind let's examine the nuance of question one and why it works.

Despite being called The Perfect *Close,* question one is not really a closing question. The question, "Does it make sense…" is NOT the same as, "Will you buy?"

"Does it make sense?" ≠ "Will you buy?"

"Does it make sense…" is not any of the common close questions of which there are infinite varieties. To elaborate, "Does it make sense…" is not:

- Will you buy?

- Will you X? (i.e. do something)

- Do you want it in green or blue? (loaded)

- Where do you want it shipped? (assumed)

- Q. Do you have it in X? A. Would you buy it if we had it in X?

- If I can do X will you buy today?

- Shall we get started on the contract?

- This is the perfect time to move forward, isn't it? (manipulative)

- This offer ends today, and you don't want to miss out do you? (manipulative)

Question one of The Perfect Close is not any form of ultimatum. We are not asking our client to DO anything. We are simply asking if a given thing (your advance) makes sense.

At its core, question one is really a **timing** question. We are asking **if the timing is right** to do something. In fact, asking with those terms is a perfectly acceptable variation of the technique. "You know Bob, is the timing right for us to talk about scheduling a site visit for you and your team?" After years of application and teaching it to others I prefer "Does it make sense..." because it has proven to be easier to remember for my students and more universal in its application. Both are fine. If the "timing" phrase feels more natural for you, use it.

There is a subtle but absolutely critical difference between asking our client to do something and asking if it makes sense to do something. Here's the difference:

Differences between traditional closes & The Perfect Close

Will you X?	Does it make sense to X?
Yes/No question on a single course of action.	Cannot reject the course of action—only the timing of it.
Timed improperly, creates pressure and tension.	Eliminates the pressure and tension risk of improperly timed questions (because it is a timing question).
May cause clients to view you as pushy and limit future communications.	Eliminates the risk that clients may see you as pushy. Keeps clients communicating throughout their buying process.
Leaves you at square one if the reply is no.	Sets up your follow-up question (question 2) if the reply is negative.
Reveals little to nothing about where the client is in their buying process.	Reveals much about where the client is within their buying process.
	Paces the sale at the rate the customer is ready to go.
	Feels facilitative to clients and makes them feel in control.

Closing Secret #16 - By asking a timing question prospects cannot reject you or your course of action, only the timing of it.

The most important distinction between the two approaches is that when you directly ask a client to do something in a polar or binary fashion (i.e. Will you X?), they are forced into a yes/no response. It is wonderful when they say "yes" and binary questions are not without their merits. However, when a client answers negatively to our binary request they have officially rejected our advance, and that leaves us back at square one. Moreover, depending on the request and how far we are mismatched from where the client is in their buying process, there is a heightened risk that we will be perceived as being pushy or self-serving (even if that is not our intention). If prospects get the impression that we are being self-serving or pushy they throttle down the rate of communication and information they share with us. In some cases they may cease communicating with us altogether.

Contrast this with question one of The Perfect Close. When we ask a client if it "makes sense" to do something, we are not actually asking them to take that step yet, but they can clearly see that is the direction we are heading. If they reply in the negative they are not rejecting the course of action, rather they are just rejecting the timing of it. Because it is a timing question this leaves you and the client emotionally on much higher ground.

Closing Secret #17
When we ask if something "makes sense" we are not asking them to do anything, but they can clearly see that is the direction we are heading.

Closing Secret #18
Regardless of a client's answer, The Perfect Close questions leave you and your client emotionally on much higher ground.

It also eliminates the risk that buyers may view you as pushy. It is impossible to get the timing of this question wrong precisely because it **IS** a timing question. This keeps clients communicating freely throughout the entire buying process and paces the sale at the rate the customer is ready to go. This improves the client's experience, makes them feel like they are much more in control, and makes your process feel facilitative.

Your client's response to question one (your ideal advance) reveals much about where the client is in their buying cycle. If they decline the timing of a modest or an extremely logical advance then it is an indicator to us that we have missed something. Again, because we didn't actually ask our client to take this step as with other types of closes, we still have options. We can probe further to discover what we missed, we might fall back to a backup advance or both depending on the circumstances.

Regardless of our client's answer, question one of The Perfect Close leaves us on emotionally higher ground with more options. So in this regard it is superior to all other closing techniques.

Regardless of the answer, it effortlessly sets up question two of The Perfect Close (which we will delve into momentarily).

You see here that there is a subtle yet very important difference between question one of The Perfect Close and other closing techniques. It is a critical nuance that you need to get right when asking this question, or you may get it wrong and not achieve the outcome you are hoping for.

Getting it Wrong

Toward the end of a frenetic quarter, a young, new member of my team contacted me regarding an opportunity he hoped to close by the end of the quarter. He reported that his prospective client had a proposal and had been through all of the steps of our selling process. So it seemed like everything was in line for an end-of-quarter close.

To seal the deal, my rep was requesting approval on a concession he hoped to offer his prospect as an incentive to get them to buy before the end of the quarter. I don't like giving concessions—especially to buy business. My experience is that at the end stage of most complex sales you have less than 10–15% control over the timing of when a deal will close. Don't get me wrong, sales cycles can definitely be shortened, but the shortening happens earlier in the sales cycle not at the end.

So a very common mistake that inexperienced professionals make is that they offer a discount or some special incentive in hopes of inducing their buyer to close sooner. There are many things wrong with this practice that I won't go into here, but the most important is that clients tend to ignore the timing requirement and see the concession as an indicator of what the offer should have been all along. The killer is that they will expect these concessions regardless of when they close, whether it is in your desired time frame or not.

Said another way, once you offer a concession, your client is expecting that concession regardless of all other factors.

My rep was excited and felt strongly that a potential concession was all that was needed. Since all of the preliminaries seemed to have been done, I directed him to use one of the classic applications of The Perfect Close which I call *Something Special*. I told him to ask, "Does it make sense for me to see if we can do something special for you if we can get everything wrapped up by the end of the quarter?" (you recognize this as question one of The Perfect Close).

Curious, my rep asked, "Well, what if he says yes? What is the special something that we might do for them?"

My reply, "We have lots of options depending on what they might value the most. Let's just see if the timing works."

Persistently my rep asked for more clarification, "Well what kinds of things are possible?"

My reply, "There are all kinds of things. We can play with the terms, the deposit, we could change the licensing scope, play with the maintenance; we could get them some users-group passes. There are a lot of directions we can take it."

Rep, "Can we get them a discount?"

Me, "Sure. Discounting is one of the options. Let's just start with the timing, and then as a second step we can determine which concession will be most effective."

Rep, "Ok. I'll call them right now. Thanks!"

A little while later I saw my rep in the hall looking disappointed. I inquired how the call had gone with his opportunity and he replied, "Your question didn't work at all."

"Oh really?" I asked, "What happened?"

Rep, "Well, I asked him your question, and he got all angry and then asked me to create a new proposal with a bigger discount on it."

Me, "Really. That's surprising. Why did he get angry?"

Rep, "He said he would let me know when he was ready to buy, and he was mad that we hadn't already offered him our best price."

Me, "So he immediately assumed that 'something special' meant a discount? That's strange."

Rep, "Yep. Now I have to create a new proposal."

It just so happened that we were testing a new phone system that would let us audit the calls of our reps for coaching purposes, so I decided to review the call myself. Here's what I found:

Instead of asking, "Does it makes sense for me to see if we can do something special for you if we can get everything wrapped up by the end of the quarter?", my rep said "If you will sign before the end of the quarter, I can get you a bigger discount."

This is wholly different than what I instructed him to say. In effect, he was asking "Will you sign before the end of the quarter if I give you a discount?" That makes the question about the action rather than about the timing. That is, he was asking "Will you or won't you do X?"

As I continued listening through the conversation I heard the client say something very interesting. He said, "I haven't even run the proposal I have now—which was supposed to be your final proposal—past our board yet, and they don't meet until the 15th of next month."

So by rephrasing the question my rep had put his prospect into a difficult position—which clearly made him angry. The prospect didn't say so on the conversation, but you could tell he felt it would be impossible for him to get the board together in the next two days for an impromptu meeting.

This guy clearly wanted our solution. It was just a question of timing.

As a sidebar, it is also bad that my rep replaced the phrase "something special" with the word "discount." This is best left undefined until we know the timing is right. Once we know that closing is possible, then we can determine what special concession will have the greatest impact.

When coaching my rep afterwards I told him I was curious why he had changed the question so dramatically even after he had written it down.

His reply was that he understood the concept and didn't reference the question at all during the call. He thought he was speeding things up by changing what was going to be a two-step process (ask about timing, then discuss "something special") down to a single question, "Will you buy if I give you a discount?"

Next I mentioned I was curious about why he went straight for "discount" instead of using the phrase "something special." Again, he felt he was upgrading the question and speeding things up by deciding in advance that the discount was the best of the options.

This was an eye opening experience for my rep that taught him the importance of following the nuance prescribed in The Perfect Close. He learned to apply it regularly, and went on to become one of my best implementers of the approach.

So what can we learn about The Perfect Close from this experience?

1. **Asking about the timing of a possible action is different than asking directly for that action.** It elicits a different response, and it feels emotionally different.

2. **The Perfect Close is a two question, two-step process.** Sometimes you will only need to use the first question. Trying to be efficient and shortcutting the process typically backfires. At the very least it reintroduces all of the risks of a direct close and eliminates all the benefits of The Perfect Close. Be patient. Your client WILL let you ask your second question. They are not going to suddenly stop talking to you mid-conversation.

3. **Stick to the recommended phraseology.** There is plenty of room in The Perfect Close to tailor it to your individual style.

However, before you do so, have a clear understanding of how your changes will affect your client's reactions. Until you have mastered this you will get the best results by sticking to the recommended phraseology.

So what happened to my young rep's deal? We ultimately won the opportunity about a month later when our contact was able to submit and get approval on our final proposal with his board, but our final offer had been adjusted to include a greater discount (as my rep had suggested was available).

There are a couple other bonus learning moments we can draw from this experience:

1. **Timing issues are not price issues.** In this particular deal it was never really about the price or additional concessions. It was a about timing. Our contact was sold with the earlier offer and was just waiting for the opportunity to get approvals and work the buying process internally. Operating in sync with the buyer's buying process would have brought the opportunity in at higher margin.

2. **Telegraphing a concession means giving that concession**. Once a client hears that a concession is possible, count on having to give that concession. By changing the phrase "something special" in my suggested phrase to "discount" my rep had ultimately committed to giving that discount. In the *Something Special* application of The Perfect Close, it is important that we come to the conversation without any particular concession in mind. Your attitude should be "Well, I don't know what my options are without talking to some folks, but if the timing is right I'll go see what I can do." We will discuss this application more below, but you'll find that *Something Special* accomplishes three important things: a) it doesn't telegraph

any kind of concession; b) it answers the timing question of what is possible; c) it positions you as an advocate for the client.

Closing Secret #19

Timing issues are not price issues.

How to Get it Right

The rest of this chapter will be about getting it right. One of the beautiful things about The Perfect Close is that you don't have to understand it for it to work. It just works. Even if you don't know why. So learn the basics, use the recommended phrases and when you have mastered the psychology, tailor it and make it your own.

The Perfect Close Model

There are only two possible outcomes of The Perfect Close question "Does it make sense to X?" Yes or no. If "Yes," then great, you just successfully executed The Perfect Close and got your advance with a single question! It's time to schedule that next step (because we know the timing is right, right?).

But... what if they say "No"?

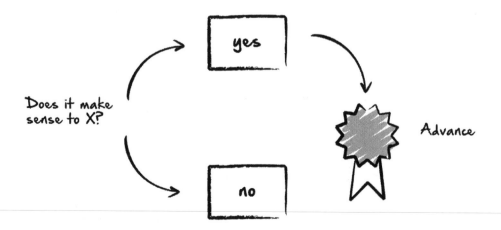

If They Say No

So what if they say, "No, it doesn't make sense to talk about doing X?" What then?

Let's explore. What have they said "no" to exactly? Have they said, "No, I will not buy?" No, because we did not ask them to buy. Did they say, "No, I will not take your action?" No, because we did not ask them to take an action.

What we asked was, "Does it make sense?"

When our client answers "no" to the question, "Does it make sense?" they are sharing important information about where they are in their buying cycle. They are sharing with us that at this moment this particular action doesn't make *sense*. That is, the **timing** is not right.

This is perfectly ok. Each client and opportunity has their own unique buying cycle with their own unique dynamics. While there are definite patterns to that process, each opportunity will have slightly different dynamics that affect the speed and timing of their process. In a future work I'll discuss the things you can do to enable and speed up this process, but for now know this: When a client answers "no" to question one, they are simply saying that the **timing** is not yet right for that step.

---

*When a client answers "no" to question one, they are simply saying that the **timing** is not yet right for that step.*

Now what? Well, if your suggested advance was a reasonable and logical one, then you must be wondering, "Hmm... I guess they're not where I thought they were. So, what **does** make sense right now?"

This is the key attitude to take into question two of The Perfect Close—figuring out what **does** make sense right now. With that in mind let's consider question two of The Perfect Close.

Question Two of The Perfect Close

Your follow-up to hearing "no" to question one is, of course, to ask question two. I will share some variations of question two in a moment, but for now your basic response will be, "Ok. What is a good next step then?"

Question two of the perfect close is:
"What is a good next step then?"

After years of using this approach myself and teaching it to others I can tell you what happens in 90% of cases—your client will simply suggest a very logical next step for advancing the sale.

Your client will simply suggest a very logical next
step for advancing the sale.

It would be hard to overstate the impact of this. The buyer is telling us what feels like a logical and natural next step **for them**. We don't have to be clairvoyant or have a perfect understanding of where they are in the buying process. In fact, we could be brand new to selling without the tiniest clue of what ought to happen next, and it will still work because the customer will suggest it for us.

Closing Secret #20

Clients will always be comfortable with their own suggested next steps.

This makes it perfect for new and inexperienced professionals. Sure, ideally, professionals will know all they need to know about their solutions and all of the steps their prospective customers might go through when traversing their own buyer's journey. If that were the case we would always know the most logical and natural next step to suggest in that buyer's journey. Yes, that would be ideal.

But the reality of it is that we all come to our positions inexperienced. No one is born with detailed knowledge about their solutions or their customer's buying process. When we attain a new position or begin a new venture we are inexperienced. In the beginning we are *all* inexperienced.

Closing Secret #21

In the beginning we are all inexperienced.

As a manager, I hire individuals that have some experience selling (sometimes not), but they generally have no experience with the solutions we offer nor all the possible dimensions that clients may go through as they make their buying decisions. Does it make sense for me to wait until my new hire has mastered all things before placing them into the field? With complex solutions, that could be a very long time indeed.

What about those starting a new venture? Perhaps they have mastered the domain knowledge in a given profession after years of schooling but have little or no experience with the selling process. Are we to expect them to now master selling before they can be successful in their given profession?

None of this is necessary. All that is necessary is a facilitative approach to advancing the sale. The Perfect Close is a Godsend for new or inexperienced professionals because it means they can become productive almost immediately without any concern that they will come off as pushy. All that is needed is to learn the questions of The Perfect Close. If they miss the mark on question one, the customer will guide them through each step when they answer question number two.

Closing Secret #22

The Perfect Close allows inexperienced professionals to be productive immediately.

Example Vignettes of The Perfect Close

Sound too easy? Let's walk through a couple of vignettes to illustrate how simple it is.

PROFESSIONAL: "Well Jeff, now that you've seen a full demonstration it's pretty common to want to see it humming in a live environment at a client site. Does it make sense for us to talk about scheduling a site visit for you?

POTENTIAL CLIENT: "No, I don't think we need that yet."

PROFESSIONAL: "Gotcha. Well what do you think would make a good next step then?"

POTENTIAL CLIENT: "Well, there are some other people here that I think would benefit from seeing this. Would it be ok if we scheduled another demonstration for them?"

PROFESSIONAL: "Sure. Let's look at some dates together."

PROFESSIONAL: "Does it make sense for us to talk about putting together a financial assessment of your current situation to see where and what the upside might be?"

POTENTIAL CLIENT: "No, I don't think so."

PROFESSIONAL: "I see. Well what do you think would make a good next step then?"

POTENTIAL CLIENT: "The assessment sounds valuable. Do you have an example of something you've prepared for another client so we can review it as a team?"

PROFESSIONAL: "Absolutely. Let's schedule some time to go over it together so you know what you're looking at, and then you can explain it to your team. Or I'd be happy to do that for you, if you like."

PROFESSIONAL: "Does it make sense for us to talk about getting your credit approved while we go through the other details together?"

POTENTIAL CLIENT: "Not at all. You're way ahead of yourself here."

PROFESSIONAL: "Ok. What do you see as a good next step then?"

POTENTIAL CLIENT: "I'm going to need to see a complete statement of work for the whole project before we do anything like that."

PROFESSIONAL: "Actually that makes great sense. I believe we've got everything we need now. Let me put that together, and let's schedule a time to go over it together to make sure we have everything right."

I'm sure you are starting to get the pattern now and are realizing how easy this can be. I've trained newcomers to my team on this in as little as five minutes. At its core it's just really very simple.

The Softening Statement

There's one element of question two that I haven't mentioned but I'm sure you noticed in all of the examples. I call it *The Softening Statement.* Did you notice that in each example after the potential client communicates that the timing is not right that our professional immediately follows with a brief understanding statement?

These statements acknowledge that you heard them, that you understand them, and it sets up question two, "What is a good next step then?"

So the formula to question two of The Perfect Close looks like:

Question 2 = Softening Statement + "What is a good next step?"

There are wide variety of possible softening statements, so practice it a few times and find a few that work for you and your style. I tend to prefer the shortest ones. Here are some examples for you that my teams have used over the years:

- Got it.
- Gotcha.
- Ok.
- I see.
- I understand.
- Mmmm...
- All right.
- Oh, ok.
- I'm tracking.
- Sounds like I missed the mark.
- Sounds like the timing is not right for that yet.
- Let's stay in sync then.
- Let's move at your pace then.

I've heard many others as well, and as I mentioned I prefer the shortest ones. I've also seen it be successful when no statement is used at all. When the understanding and rapport is already present it isn't necessary to restate it. It is all conveyed in the eyes and in the feeling that is already present. The closest to this in the list above would be "Mmmm..." (the sound conveying "I understand.").

As previously noted, intent matters more than technique. So if you have conveyed good intent don't get hung up on the technique. Do what is natural for you, and then ask for a good next step.

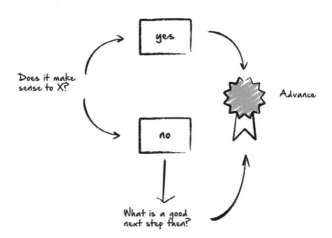

So here we see The Perfect Close model with both questions incorporated showing how The Perfect Close produces an advance. I have studied it with my own teams, and if you are in front of a genuine prospective client, this simple model by itself will produce a successful advance 90-95% of the time. Try it yourself and keep track. I would love to hear about your experiences at PureMuir.com.

Variations to Improve Your Success

95% is excellent but I have to admit it's not *perfect*. So what I'd like to share with you now is some variations of The Perfect Close that will help you shore up that final 5%.

The Suggestion

The first variation of The Perfect Close is called *The Suggestion*. It is a minor tweak to question number one. This is especially helpful when your prospective client does not have much purchasing experience and does not have a clear vision of how they will go about evaluating options.

These prospects absolutely need your help in navigating their buyer's journey, and this variation is one method you can use to shorten the sales cycle for them.

This variation requires that you have a clear understanding of the most common or logical sequence that your prospects go through when purchasing your kind of product or service. That is because you are going to suggest that path with each advance (if you jumped ahead to this chapter, you'll find more about this topic in Chapter 8).

In this variation you are simply going to add one additional statement before asking question number one. That statement is some variation of:

"Other clients at this stage typically take X as a next step in their evaluation."

Here, X is the advance that you are about to check the timing of with question one. For example:

"Other clients at this stage typically schedule a meeting between us and your team so we can get their input and participation on what would help them the most. Does it make sense for us to schedule a meeting with your team, so we can get their input on what would be most beneficial for them?"

This variation changes the first question formula to look like this:

"Clients at this stage typically do X" + "Does it makes sense for us to X?"

Here are a couple more examples to give you the feel of it:

"Other clients at this stage typically schedule time to watch a procedure where the device is being put in place and then have a follow-up discussion with the surgical team. Does it make sense for us to talk about scheduling a time for you to see the procedure at a client site?"

"Other clients at this stage typically have us perform a workflow analysis so we can see where you'll get the most improvement. Does it make sense for us to talk about scheduling a workflow analysis so we can see where the best efficiencies can be gained?"

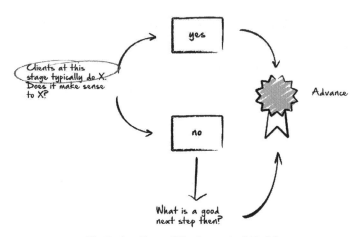

The Perfect Close – "The Suggestion" Model

It's very straight forward. It's basically, "At this stage others typically do X. Does it make sense to X?"

In this way you can walk your client through each stage of the process if they are in unfamiliar territory. Yet (and this is an important distinction), we are still asking and advancing at a pace that is comfortable to our prospect. This generates a ton of value for unsure buyers, and perhaps, a lot of gratitude.

One final comment on this variation, both you and your prospect will get a lot of value from mapping all of the common steps at once. Then the path will be clear to both of you, and you can simply help your client go through each step, if that is the same path they wish to follow.

The Fall Back

The next variation of The Perfect Close, which we touched on in Chapter 8, is called *The Fall Back* and it is important that you learn it. You will use it any time you are not able to get your ideal advance.

In this variation you *fall back* to a secondary or back-up advance if your ideal advance proves unobtainable. You do this by suggesting it after your ideal advance fails and before you ask, "What is a good next step then?"

This variation typically requires a suggestion component, as in the example above, so it will be beneficial if you have a good understanding of the typical process clients go through when purchasing your type of solution. This is why we prepared ourselves by doing the exercise in Chapter 8.

It looks like this:

Question One: "Does it makes sense to do X?"

Question Two (if question one fails): "Clients at this stage typically do X. Does it make sense to do X?"

Question Three (if question two fails): "What's a good next step then?"

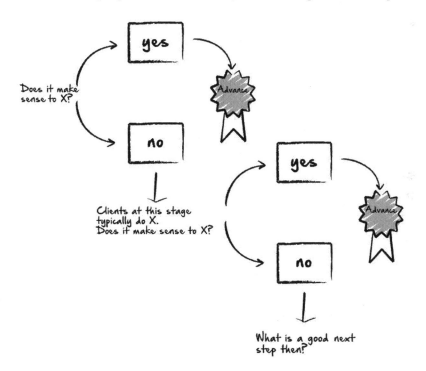

The Perfect Close – "The Fall-Back" Model

Here are some examples:

PROFESSIONAL: "Nathan, does it make sense for us to talk about doing a workflow analysis so we can see where the best efficiencies can be gained?"

PROSPECTIVE CLIENT: "Mmm… I don't think so."

PROFESSIONAL: "Ok. A lot of folks at this stage will schedule a demonstration for their whole team so they can get their reaction and feedback. Does it make sense for us to schedule a demonstration for your whole team, so they can see it in action?"

PROSPECTIVE CLIENT: "That's just what I was thinking."

PROFESSIONAL: "Isaac, does it make sense for us to talk about getting your credit approved while we go through the other details together?"

PROSPECTIVE CLIENT: "Oooh… I don't know," (body language says he's clearly uncomfortable).

PROFESSIONAL: "All right. Well, most clients at this stage will complete the financial goals part of the plan and then schedule a time for us to go over it together and talk through some options. Does it make sense for us to schedule that?"

PROSPECTIVE CLIENT: "That would be perfect. Then I can go over it with Terri before we meet again."

PROFESSIONAL: "Hey Kelly, does it make sense for us to schedule some time for our technical teams to get together so we can get a clearer picture of the requirements?"

PROSPECTIVE CLIENT: "Mmm… I don't think so."

PROFESSIONAL: "Gotcha. Most clients at this stage will have us do a site assessment so we can see what we can leverage of your existing infrastructure. Does it make sense for us to schedule a time to come do a site assessment for you?"

PROSPECTIVE CLIENT: "I don't know about that..."

PROFESSIONAL: "I see. What would you say is a good next step then?"

PROSPECTIVE CLIENT: "What I'd like to do is have you meet our CIO first. Would that be ok?"

In theory you can fall back to as many secondary/back-up advances as you have planned. In practical application, however, any more than one or two tends to come off as agenda-pushing. It is definitely useful to prepare many fall-back or secondary advances so you can select the most appropriate one for the situation if you need to fall back, but I would recommend actually only verbalizing one or two when using this variation.

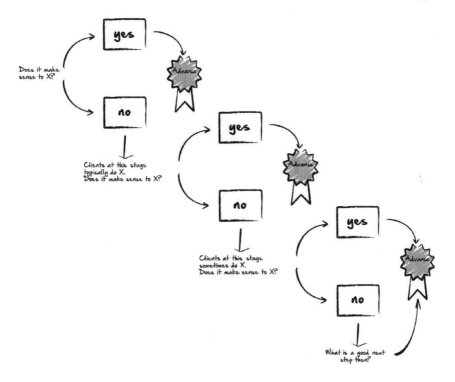

The Perfect Close – Multi-stage "The Fall-Back" Model

The Add-On

The *Add-On* variation is the reverse of the Fall-Back variation. Instead of falling back to our alternate advances, we are going to add them on.

In this variation once you achieve success with your ideal advance you continue on to suggest one of the additional alternate advances you have prepared.

This variation typically requires a suggestion component as in the example above so it will be beneficial for you to have a good understanding of the typical process clients go through when purchasing your type of solution. As with the other variations, you can further prepare yourself by doing the exercise in Chapter 8.

Once again, all we are doing here is pacing the sales cycle to match the client's buying cycle. So if the client is ready to move forward at a faster pace than we were originally thinking, we can match that perfectly by incrementally adding advances.

The Add-On variation has one more unique element at the end that differs from the Fall-Back. Instead of falling back to "What is a good next step then?" we ask "Are there any other logical steps we should be taking right now?"

This gives our client the chance to suggest any action steps that are logical to them that we may not have considered.

Here is what the model looks like:

Question One: "Does it makes sense to do X?"

Question Two (after question one succeeds): "Clients at this stage very often also do X. Does it make sense to do X?"

Question Three (after question two also succeeds): "We can also do X if it makes sense. Does it make sense to do X?"

Question Four (if question three fails): "Ok. Are there any other logical steps we should be taking right now?"

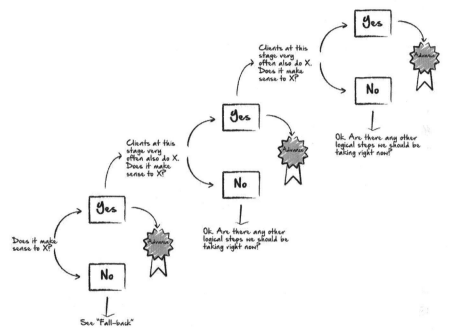

The Perfect Close – "The Add-On" Model

Here are some examples:

PROFESSIONAL: "Hey Don, does it make sense for us to talk about putting together a financial assessment of your current situation?"

PROSPECTIVE CLIENT: "Oh yes. We need to see that."

PROFESSIONAL: "Great. I'll schedule that with your team. A lot of clients at this stage will also have us present those results to their board. Does it make sense for us to schedule a time to present the results?"

PROSPECTIVE CLIENT: "Oh yes, that would be extremely helpful. The best time would be two weeks from now at our board meeting. Is that too soon?"

PROFESSIONAL: "Let's plan for it, and we will burn the midnight oil so we can make your meeting. Some groups want to see our HQ where all the magic happens. Do you have any interest in visiting the HQ?"

PROSPECTIVE CLIENT: "Nah, that isn't necessary."

PROFESSIONAL: "Got it. Are there any other logical steps we should be taking right now?"

PROSPECTIVE CLIENT: "Yeah. I know Chris is going to want to see some references. Can you get me a list of clients he can call if he wants?"

PROFESSIONAL: "Absolutely. I'll put everything together for us."

PROFESSIONAL: "Hey Regan, does it make sense for us to talk about scheduling a demo for the rest of your team so we can get their input and participation?"

PROSPECTIVE CLIENT: "Yes. We need everyone on board."

PROFESSIONAL: "Great. Let's look at some possible dates. A lot of clients at this stage will also have us schedule time for both our technical teams to discuss the dynamics around the conversion. Does it make sense for us to schedule our tech people to meet?"

PROSPECTIVE CLIENT: "Absolutely. My guys are worried about that. That's a great idea."

PROFESSIONAL: "Ok. I'll get some dates my team is open, and we can coordinate. I think we have everything we need for a proposal. Does it make sense for me to put together a preliminary proposal so you can get a feel for the scope of the project?"

PROSPECTIVE CLIENT: "Yes. That would be really helpful."

PROFESSIONAL: "Ok. I have some homework here. Are there any other logical steps we should be taking right now?"

PROSPECTIVE CLIENT: "Well, is there any chance I can see a copy of your standard agreement? Our legal team can be kind of slow sometimes."

PROFESSIONAL: "Absolutely. I know what you're talking about. I'll get you a copy of that too so your legal team can start reviewing it."

Obviously this is the best and most fun of all the variations because in a smooth and Zen-like fashion we just keep piling on advances until we've matched the pace at which our client wants to go. This is yet another way we can shorten the sales cycle. Instead of assuming that each client will progress at the same rate and preparing just a single advance (or worse, no advance), we can pace it at exactly their comfort level.

Unlike the Fall-Back variation, there doesn't seem to be a point of diminishing returns for Add-On Advances. The second example above is an excerpt of an actual, real-life conversation. My team and I were hoping to parlay our demo with a small group into a larger demo that could include many more important players who we knew would be involved in the decision. We never dreamed that sending a copy of the contract would emerge as a realistic next step in our sales process. In fact, it's possible that if we had suggested sending contracts as our first ideal advance, that Regan (not the client's real name) might have been put off. But instead, by diplomatically pacing it at the rate the client was ready to receive it, we scored an amazing four advances (one of which we hadn't even thought of ourselves)!

The Reverse Order

The last variation of The Perfect Close is called *The Reverse Order*. It is the most open of all the variations and comes with both advantages and disadvantages. In this variation you reverse the questions and ask question two of The Perfect Close first and question one of The Perfect Close second.

It looks like this:

Question One: "What would you say is a good next step?"

Question Two (if the client is stumped): "Does it make sense for us to X?'"

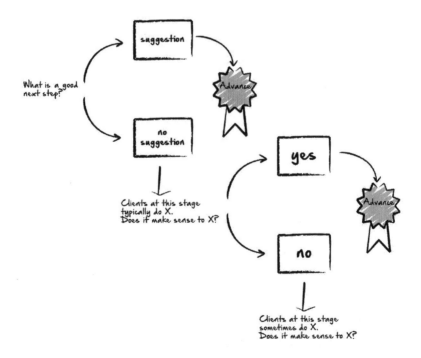

The Perfect Close – "The Reverse Order" Model

Here are two examples of possible outcomes:

PROFESSIONAL: "Well Mike, what would you say is a good next step?"

PROSPECTIVE CLIENT: "I was thinking it would be helpful to talk to an existing client here in Australia."

PROFESSIONAL: "No problem. I'll set it up for us. Let's look at your calendar."

PROFESSIONAL: "Well Mike, what would you say is a good next step?"

PROSPECTIVE CLIENT: "Uh, nothing comes to mind really."

PROFESSIONAL: "Well, other clients at this stage typically want to see it live in operation. Does it make sense for us to talk about getting you out to a client site?"

This variation has advantages as well as drawbacks. On the plus side, because it is wide open, it opens up more possibilities than you might have considered with your own suggested advances. This, in and of itself, could be good or bad. A client-suggested advance does not necessarily mean it will be the best advance for them or for you.

On the flip side, because the suggestion is theirs, the client will feel like they are more in control with this variation than any of the other variations. This can be good if you have a strong-willed individual who clearly knows what they want and likes to be in the driver's seat or context dictates that you are as open as possible in order to maintain rapport.

Reverse Order is the least assertive of all the variations. Most clients appreciate helpful facilitation toward their desired outcome. However, a small percentage of individuals can be put off by the slightest assertion. These individuals are not typically decision-makers, but this approach may be most appropriate for them.

The biggest drawback with this variation is that the client may not be able to come up with a good next step, or any kind of a next step. We can still save a situation like that with question two in this variation but it is not as elegant as the normal model.

This is the model to use if you have not yet learned your customer's typical buying process or you are not sure what an appropriate next step might be. You should be investing time to learn that process so you can use the other models. In most cases however, your customer will suggest a next step that is appropriate for their pace, and those steps will ultimately teach you the elements of your customers buying process.

The Reverse Order is best used when you are not sure what an appropriate next step might be and when it is important that the client feel that they are strongly in control of the process, and when they clearly have a vision and path of how they want things done.

Classic Application of The Perfect Close—Something Special

There are unlimited possibilities and variations of The Perfect Close. There is one application of The Perfect Close that is used far more frequently than others. I call it *Something Special*.

If you are involved in sales in any way then I'm sure you are familiar with the pressures associated with reaching end-of-quarter or perhaps even end-of-month quotas. It is unfortunate that these pressures often give rise to many dysfunctional selling practices. One common tactic is to offer a concession of some kind in order to close the sale before the end of the month or quarter.

End-of-quarter discounts are essentially trading margin for timing. As previously mentioned, I am not an advocate of discounting in an attempt to accelerate timing. However, having worked for a publicly traded company for almost two decades, I do understand the dynamics involved. In some cases revenue recognized in this quarter may actually be more valuable to the company than that same revenue the following quarter. So as you can imagine, I have a long history of executive management encouraging accelerated sales every quarter, often times by whatever means possible.

I recall a particular quarter where I had on my office whiteboard exactly ten opportunities for new business that were all in play. One of these opportunities was ripe and ready to go but the others were somewhere in the middle of their buying process. Two weeks before the end of the quarter we received the word from above—this was a particularly challenging quarter, and we needed to use all legal means possible to bring in more business.

I was encouraged to offer discounts, which I did, to all ten accounts as an inducement to close before month's end. Each account knew that the discount was conditional upon receiving agreements before end of quarter.

One deal signed. The very deal that was already at the closing stage before we had decided to start offering discounts. The remaining nine accounts chose to continue their evaluation rather than take advantage of the discounts. Naturally we continued working these into the subsequent quarter, and ultimately we closed seven more of the original ten for a total of eight out of ten.

Unfortunately, on every opportunity there was this awkward conversation about whether or not they could get the same discount they saw the previous quarter. "If it was worth it to you before, why isn't it worth it to you now?" they would ask. Resisting the request would sometimes create a tangible erosion of goodwill. Ironically, near the end of the very next quarter I found myself in a repeat fire drill of the previous quarter where discounts were encouraged to close business. Naturally I used this opportunity to provide the discounts I had before and all ended well—though with lower margins.

And thus I found myself having unintentionally trained my buyers to wait until the end of the quarter in order to get concessions, but that's another story for another day.

It was this dynamic that caused me to think creatively about how to offer concessions. There must be a way, I thought, to see if a deal can really close by end of quarter without telegraphing the concession and having to give that concession later even if they couldn't close by EOQ.

And thus *Something Special* was born.

Something Special Application

Something Special is really just a standard Perfect Close question that reveals the client's timing without telegraphing a concession. This variation is helpful for end of quarter and upselling situations. Many professionals have told me that this one close is among the most valuable things they've ever learned in sales. You be the judge. Here it is verbatim:

"Does it make sense for me to see if we can do something special for you if we can get everything wrapped up by the end of the quarter?"

"Does it make sense for me to see if we can do something special for you if we can get everything wrapped up by the end of the quarter?"

Naturally you adapt the time frame to suit your situation. Otherwise I recommend you use it verbatim.

In the Something Special application of The Perfect Close it is important that we come to the conversation without any particular concession in mind. Determining exactly what the client deems as *special* will require another step and further conversation.

Your attitude should be: "Well, I don't know what my options are without talking to some folks, but if the timing is right I'll go see what I can do for us."

The beauty of this approach is if the timing isn't right for the client, you will never have to discuss what that "something special" might have been, and your margins are preserved going into the next period.

If the buyer says that it "IS possible to wrap things up" within your timeframe, then you have a couple of options:

1. Ask what they would find most valuable. Not guaranteeing anything until you first talk with others inside your organization.

2. Tell them you will go see what you can do and that you will report back. Then go discuss your options with your organization or supervisor.

These two options are not mutually exclusive. I prefer to use them both. The only time you would want to skip option one is if it is possible that the client will suggest concession options that you know you won't be able to satisfy. In that case, asking will only set an expectation that you can't meet.

While concessions vary by industry, some common ones involve delivery, training details, additional services, optional modules, maintenance, payment options, and the list goes on. I have often found that my client's preference for a concession was not what I was expecting. Based on the dynamics within a given organization, clients often value concessions on services more than a discount on the basic price. Knowing this gives you much more flexibility in crafting your offer, and if a client values something that has a lower hard cost to your company, it's a real win-win.

Here are some examples of how your conversation might go:

PROFESSIONAL: "Gary, does it make sense for me to see if we can do something special for you if we can get everything wrapped up by the end of the quarter?"

PROSPECTIVE CLIENT: "I don't think so. Our CEO is out until after the holidays. We wouldn't be able to do anything until he's back."

[Margin Preserved]

PROFESSIONAL: "Hey Gary, does it make sense for me to see if we can do something special for you if we can get everything wrapped up by the end of the quarter?"

PROSPECTIVE CLIENT: "Maybe. What did you have in mind?"

PROFESSIONAL: "Well, I don't know what my options are without talking to some folks, but if the timing is right I'll go see what I can do for us."

PROSPECTIVE CLIENT: "If the offer is right I think we can do something. Go find out what you can do."

PROFESSIONAL: "Hey Gary, does it make sense for me to see if we can do something special for you if we can get everything wrapped up by the end of the quarter?"

PROSPECTIVE CLIENT: "Hmmm, what are you thinking?"

PROFESSIONAL: "Well, I don't know what my options are without talking to our CEO, but if we can actually do something this quarter he said he would be willing to work with clients."

PROSPECTIVE CLIENT: "If the offer's good enough we're ready to do something. Why don't you find out what he's thinking?"

PROFESSIONAL: "You got it. Just to speed the process up a bit; is there any part of the proposal that you would get more value out of than another? I'll see if that's an area we can play in for us."

PROSPECTIVE CLIENT: "There is. Michelle is concerned that some of our folks will need more training than usual, so anything you could do in that area will make me hero with her. From my perspective, it would be great if there was something you could do with the maintenance. Lowering it or starting it later would be great. So that's it, maintenance and training. See if there is something he can do there. Thanks."

Something Special accomplishes three important things:

1. It doesn't telegraph any kind of concession or the size of that concession.

2. It reveals if the client is able to do something within your suggested time frame.

3. It positions you as an advocate for the client. You are doing all this on their behalf.

If you've ever found yourself on the end-of-quarter discount rollercoaster, you will appreciate how Something Special preserves both revenues and your commissions.

Best Practice Principles for Using The Perfect Close

By this time you should have a clear understanding of the model and just how simple it is. Many individuals have learned the model in less time than it took you to read this chapter. Let's wrap up this section by discussing how to best use The Perfect Close in your daily selling and business development activities.

- **Initially, use the suggested phraseology.** There is plenty of room in The Perfect Close to tailor it to your individual style. However, before you do, have a clear understanding of how your changes will affect your client's reactions. Until you have mastered this you will get the best results by sticking to the recommended phraseology. Once you have a good understanding how and why The Perfect Close works, a whole world of possible variations will open up to you. I would love to hear about your application and innovations at PureMuir.com.

- **Know your prospective clients typical buying process.** The Perfect Close will work even if you aren't completely sure of your prospect's buying process. However, when you have a clear understanding of your clients' typical buying process you can help them further by suggesting logical and productive advances that will eventually reach the outcomes they seek.

- **Prepare advances before every sales encounter.** Good selling depends on good planning more than any other single factor. Plan an ideal advance and several alternative or back-up advances before every sales encounter. This insures you the ability and flexibility to utilize the Fall-Back and Add-On variations of The Perfect Close and match your sales efforts with your prospect's pace.

- **Use The Perfect Close in every sales encounter.** You should plan on advancing your opportunity in some way on every sales encounter. The Perfect Close is essentially a risk-free way of testing and then asking for that advance. Because the process is virtually risk-free there is no downside to using it on every encounter. You will quickly master The Perfect Close—and closing in general—by using the formula for all of your closes. Like diets, the most successful approach to closing is the one you can stick to. Instead of learning a different close for each situation, master one close for all situations.

- **Use the Fall-Back variation every time your ideal advance falls short.** When your client responds that it doesn't make sense to take your ideal advance, suggest another one. You can still end with, "What's a good next step then?" Falling back to an alternate or back-up advance simply increases the chances that a productive advance will be the outcome of your meeting.

- **Use the Add-On variation every time your ideal advance succeeds.** When your client accepts your ideal advance, make sure you are moving at the right pace by asking if it makes sense for them to consider one of your alternate advances. Again, because there is no risk associated with using The Perfect Close you are able to potentially accelerate the pace without adding tension or appearing pushy.

Conclusion

Congratulations! You just learned The Perfect Close. With a little practice you can become proficient with the approach in less time than it took you to read this chapter. If you jumped right to this chapter to jumpstart your closing skills, I encourage you to now complete the rest of the book so that you can obtain its maximum benefit.

Combining what you have learned in this chapter with the principles covered in the previous chapters will shorten your sales cycle, maximize the impact of each meeting, and advance your sales in a way that differentiates you from your competition.

Having illustrations of The Perfect Close model can help accelerate your understanding and mastery of the approach. You can download a copy The Perfect Close Model at PureMuir.com.

The Perfect Close has made a tremendous difference in my life and the lives of many others. It is so simple that I encourage you to invest the small amount of time it takes to practice it. You won't find a better payoff of your time. In the next chapter we will pull together everything you have learned into one clear picture so your mastery of The Perfect Close is complete.

CHAPTER 13

Putting It All Together - The Perfect Close for Your Next Meeting in 7 Easy Steps

"A set of organized steps that align with the buyer's buying process will help a sales professional become more engaged in that process, more aware of the buyer's actions, and better informed as to your opportunity to close the sale."

–Michael Nick

N ow, let's put together everything you've learned into seven simple steps. Use this section as a checklist for your next sales encounter.

Get out your forms or a blank sheet of paper and a pen because it's time to commit your plan to paper.

Here are the seven steps:

1. Research Your Client

2. Determine Your Value Proposition

3. Define Your Questions

4. Determine Your Advances

5. Define Your Unexpected Value

6. Create Your Agenda

7. Prepare Your Mindset

Putting It All Together

STEP 1 - Research Your Client · Determine Your Value Proposition · Define Your Questions · Determine Your Advances · Define Your Unexpected Value · Create Your Agenda · Prepare Your Mindset

STEP 1 - Research Your Client

Use the questions and forms in Chapter 10 to research your client. This helps us better understand the client's situation, determine what we know and don't know, and how we might best create value for this client.

STEP 2 - Determine Your Value Proposition

Use what you learned in Chapter 7 to identify what your value is to this particular client. This step answers the first of The Three Magic Pre-call Questions, "Why should this client see me?"

STEP 3 - Define Your Questions

Questions help you gather information and add value. Use what you learned in Chapters 9 and 10 to determine what more you need to know in order to help this client, as well as how you can deliver value to them by asking High-Value Questions.

STEP 4 - Determine Your Advances

Use the brainstorming exercise you completed in Chapter 8 to determine your Ideal Advance and Secondary Advances. Remember that they should: 1. Be specific and measurable. 2. Center on the action the prospect will take. 3. Move the sale forward. 4. Be reasonable from the prospect's perspective. After choosing your Ideal Advance and Secondary Advances, write out The Perfect Close Phrase for each one. Write them verbatim so you'll be able to recall the phrasing in the heat of the moment. This step answers the second of The Three Magic Pre-call Questions, "What do I want the client to do?"

STEP 5 - Define Your Unexpected Value

Review what you learned in Chapter 9 about unexpected value and what customers value most. Then determine how you will add unexpected value on this encounter. It will likely come from one of these seven categories:

1. Deliver Insight

2. Employ Powerful Questions

3. Help Them Better Understand Their Needs

4. Help Them See the Path to Success

5. Share New Ideas

6. Deliver Education

7. Share News, Trigger Events, and Insights from Their Industry

This step answers the third of The Three Magic Pre-call Questions, "How can I provide value on this encounter?"

STEP 6 - Create Your Agenda

Use what you learned in Chapter 11 to craft an agenda. Be sure to collaborate with your client and articulate your Stated Meeting Objective. As you conduct your meeting, stick to the agenda that you and your client defined while remaining flexible. At the designated time address the obvious action items then use The Perfect Close phrase you created for your Ideal Advance. If you meet with success use the *Add-On* approach you learned in Chapter 12, if not use the *Fall-Back* approach you learned in the same chapter. Near the end of the meeting review the agreed upon action items. Cover what needs to be done, who specific tasks are assigned to, and when they will be completed. Then, establish the date and time of the next meeting.

STEP 7 - Prepare Your Mindset

Before your meeting, take advantage of the exercises and techniques you learned in Chapter 3 to ensure that your non-verbal communication sends all the right signals. Integrate your Intention Statement into your introduction or somewhere early in your meeting.

Conclusion

You now have a repeatable process for preparing for every sales encounter and advancing the sale. With a little practice it will become a habit and then you will not only become more successful, for you, success will become predictable.

A Final Word

You now know how to execute The Perfect Close. You know how to ask yourself the three magic pre-call questions to ensure that each meeting is as effective as it can be, and you've learned how to prepare and add unexpected value in every meeting.

You have also learned the concepts, principles and science that explain why these techniques work. Together, these form an approach to closing business—the approach I call the The Perfect Close.

So you've learned some stuff. Good stuff.

If you take action on what you've learned here you'll have a simple approach to closing that will serve you your entire life. It won't cause you to have to change your personality or become something you are not. You won't have to be pushy or manipulative. It will be in complete alignment with your personal values. And, most importantly, because it eliminates the tension and stress related to closing, the whole process will be more enjoyable not only for you but also for your prospective clients.

By providing value on each and every encounter your clients will feel more educated and in control. The process will turn you into a trusted advisor and differentiate you from your competition. Ultimately, you will achieve more success.

But there is a nobler meaning to this work.

Allow me to share one more experience. On a lengthy return flight I sat next to a young, ambitious salesperson. We'll call him Ace (not his real name). He looked sharp. You could tell right from the get-go, he was aggressive. In fact, he looked just a little bit intimidating. Although he was professional, the way he carried himself caused me to hesitate a bit. I found myself thinking, "I wonder what this guy's capable of? Seems like he might be willing to take advantage of someone in order to get what he wants."

As we settled in for the long flight we struck up a conversation. He was dynamic. He shared the details about his company, the solutions he sold, and with a little pride that he was their most successful new hire ever. He stated his aspirations to be their top salesperson, "I really want to kill it! I want to be number one at this company, and I'm willing to do whatever it takes to accomplish that."

I revealed to him that I managed a sales force, and I complimented him on his passion. As we became more acquainted, we shared more about our companies and our circumstances. Eventually, Ace shed his rock-star veneer, and we began to discuss the challenges that each of us was facing.

"My company can't support my sales," he said. "I bring in the business, and then they can't get my clients happy."

"Why can't they make them happy?" I asked.

"These deals are complicated," he replied. "I have to do special stuff to make them happen, and they need to make it work."

"Do you involve your team when there is a special requirement?" I followed up.

"Sometimes." He added, "But I don't always have time for that. These are big deals, and they should be grateful I'm bringing them in."

I asked, "What does your implementation team think?"

"They hate me, but that's their problem. My job is to bring in revenue."

Then, "What happens to the client when they can't make them happy?"

"That's the problem! They get mad (not the words he used) and complain to everyone!"

"And you don't see a challenge with that?" I asked.

"Look, I have to focus on selling. I can't be the implementation department and development and support. I need to sell."

Eventually, we started discussing his sales process and what he found challenging with that. He confessed that despite winning a lot of business there were many deals he should have won, but didn't. Complaining, "they become ridiculously complicated." When I asked what he meant by that, he explained, "They start asking for legal guarantees, or pilot projects, or some kind of proof that they're getting everything. They want to talk or visit with a million clients, or see the products over and over again. Other clients don't do all that. I don't know why it keeps happening."

"It sounds like you may be unintentionally telegraphing a message you don't want, and your prospects are reacting to that." I suggested.

He reacted with surprise, "Telegraphing a message? What message?"

"That you don't really care if they achieve their objectives or not. Is that possible?" I asked.

He paused for a minute. I could see the wheels turning in his mind.

Then he said, "Well, I really don't care if they achieve their objectives. That's their responsibility—not mine."

"I see."

"My job is to get them the stuff they need so they CAN get there. I'm not guaranteeing they WILL get there." He trailed off...

I asked him if he was in a place where he could receive some feedback. He said he was, so I shared this: "People can tell when you don't care. Even people who aren't as smart as you. They can tell you don't care about them, and so they don't do business with you. Or, if they want your solution bad enough they make you jump through a bunch of hoops to make sure they'll really get what you're promising—because they can see that you don't really care whether they're successful or not. You just want a sale."

He didn't take it well. For about forty-five minutes we did our own thing. Then out of the blue he said, "Do you really think people think I don't care? Do you think that's what's causing my problem?"

I shared with him everything you learned in Chapter 3. It was a lengthy and interesting conversation because he was not completely open. As we landed (and without being in complete agreement) he cut to the chase and admitted, "I really don't care about their outcomes very much, James. I think it's their responsibility. But I can see there might be something going on here that's affecting me. How can I telegraph the good messages I want?"

"There's really just one way," I replied. "Actually care. Take some time and think about it a bit, and I think you'll find that you do actually care. And when you approach your opportunities with that mindset, you'll find that not only will you make more sales, you'll make lifelong friends as well."

That is the deeper meaning of this work and the final secret. I know The Perfect Close will help you become more successful because it has helped me and many others to whom I've taught it—including Ace. But in my opinion this final truth is more valuable than all of that.

Ace and I traded contact information and have kept in touch to this day. Ace found that changing his intent made a big difference for him. Not only did he sell more, but he felt more fulfilled while doing it. It solved his challenges both inside and outside his company. He went on to become number one in his company—just as he planned—and then repeated the process at an even bigger company.

My own personal transformation as a salesperson mirrors Ace's. While I was trying to "kill it" and break all the records at my company I stumbled across Mahan Khalsa's work, *Let's Get Real or Let's Not Play*. His work had a tremendous impact on my thinking. I owe him a debt of gratitude, and so, this book is dedicated to him. Mahan authored the phrase, "Intent counts more than technique." In this book I have endeavored to share with you some of the science that explains why that is true.

The most sublime truth is that to *convey* good intent you have to *have* good intent.

Becoming a better person will make you a better salesperson. And the amazing thing is that you will find joy in becoming both.

I urge you to internalize and master the principles and techniques within these pages. Doing so will grant you a happier, more fulfilling career and life. I look forward to hearing about your success.

—*James Muir*

Help Others By Leaving a Review!

I sincerely hope you have enjoyed and benefited from this book. I am on a mission to take the dysfunction out of sales and teach sales and service professionals how being genuinely authentic actually creates the highest levels of success and happiness.

Please help others to learn more about how they can improve their approach to closing. The best way is simply to share it with your friends and colleagues. But there is another way we can reach even more people. If you write a simple review on Amazon, you can help hundreds or perhaps even thousands of other readers to make a buying decision that will improve their lives. Like you, they work hard for every penny they spend on books. With your information and encouragement you can help them focus on the right things and take action right away.

In your review share anything you think will be useful to others. Here are a few suggestions to help:

- Why did you decide read this book?

- What did you like most about this book?

- What makes this book different from others you have read?

- Did it give you practical ways to apply the info it provides? If so, share what you are going to be doing differently because you read it.

- What kinds of readers do you think would benefit most reading this book?

The best time to write a review is immediately after you've read the book while everything is still fresh in your mind. Please head over to Amazon.com and write a quick review right now.

Acknowledgments

T his work would have never happened without the support, teaching, and encouragement provided by so many individuals. It would be impossible to acknowledge them all—especially all of the thought leaders and authors that have influenced my thinking throughout the years.

I want to say thanks to those who have been so helpful to me in the completion of this book. I am a lucky person to have so many individuals willing to help me both personally and professionally.

To my wife and love of my life Marin Muir for all your encouragement and patience during the early mornings and late nights while I was learning this process, creating workshops, speeches, and writing. To Lesley Kontowicz for all your feedback, opinions, and marvelous editing work. To Kelly Skeen for your undying support and encouragement. To Jeff Mildon for your inspiration and example—I want to be like you.

To Tom Anderson for your consistent and methodical feedback. To Rick Hays for your energy, advice, and for just being fun. To Tim Eggena and David Harrell for offering the broadest most far-reaching comments and delivering a non-sales perspective (I could write two more books with your feedback—thank you!) To Steve Roberts for being the first of my peers willing to review my work—you changed my book for the better. To Tera Roy for pushing me to be more inspirational in my writing.

To Jim Thompson for your frank and candid reactions. To Kelli Castellano for pushing me to make the project more of a shocking and paradigm-shifting work. To Michelle Denison for your steady and sensible feedback—you are a rock. To Mike Swim for your excellent critique and shared experience. To Spencer Adams for your straight-shooter advice. To Mont Linkenauger, Monty Skillingstad, and Mires Quigley for your perspective and recommendations on how I could make things better—I applied them all.

To Monica Postell for your bubbly enthusiasm and extreme flip-charting abilities. To Patti Peets for your undying friendship and passion. To Ken Kontowicz for being my eternal friend—we are brothers.

I want to express my appreciation to all those who provided me with invaluable feedback via Facebook:

Jay Kurts, Ken Thoreson, Laura Posey, Miles Austin, Deb Calvert, Gerhard Gschwandtner, Mark Hunter, Brian Smith, Steven Rosen, Lee Salz, Tina LoSasso, Tibor Shanto, Trish Bertuzzi, Andy Paul, Jill Konrath, Anthony Iannarino, Jeff Shore, Jeb Blount, Mike Weinberg, John Spence, David Brock, Michael Nick, Leanne Hoagland Smith, Mark Hunter, John Tighe, Koka Sexton, Ricardo Gulko, Robert Terson, Art Sobczak, Nan Hruby, Lisa Beaumont, Alicia Puede, John MacLeod, Letitia McQuade, Veronica Downing, Cory Hansen, Jeff Waldron, Dennis Herman, Jonathan Shivers, Kim Avant, Jeff Day, Gary Hynden, Todd Reihing, Darwin Wong, Scott Atlas, Rob Davis, Michele Iglesias Schanbacher, Noah Hopping, Patty Rutherford, Robert Davis, Scott Atlas, Skip Johnson, Vanessa DiMantova, Scott Merryman, Jim Hollis, Dan Royal, Matt Stoker, Mike Sweeney, Monica Durazo, Aaron Allsop, Ben Quirk, Julie Whitehead, Hilerie Coleman, Sally Barre, Leslie Peabody, Dennis Allsop, Ed Oakley, Michael Brown, Alyson Stone, Lisa Van Rooyen, Rachel Romaszewski, Jentri King, Dan Aldridge, Javier Coles, Traci Wolbert, Steven Ford, Kim Root, Duane Peck, Dan Aldridge, Dave Fotiadis, Lori White, LeAnn Parratt, Nate Anderson, Krissy Klein, Brian Thorell, and Jonathan Shivers.

Special thanks to Isaac Pigott for your genius input and teaching me social media.

Big shout out to my many friends and helpers at NextGen Healthcare, thank you:

Nathan Pratt, Brian Sauers, Regan Costello, Chris Beard, Danny B. O'Very, Gary Hinz, Jared Muir, John Longley, Kelli Otremba, Kevin Maguire, Lisa Kirk Shepps, Maria Walker, Mark Melfa, Gary Voydanoff, Matt Robinson, Jamie Smolin, Josh Fleishman, Greg Uhde, Kevin Scott, Justin Mitts, Erica James, Conni Andrews, Dan Staszcuk, Mike Lovett, Gene Gallogly, Jonathan Harmantas, Brad Layne, Scott Atlas, Don Martin, Jaclyn O'Neal, Nick Bianco, Gil Reichert, Paul Bergeson, Jamey Christensen, Matt Barlup, Maria Walker, Terri Chamberlain, Reid Storch, Dave Woskobnick, James Taylor, Darwin Wong, Craig Sturgeon, Don Martin, Lindsay Salvatore, Cherie Holmes-Henry, Tom Farmer, Jon Brucato, Jerry Shultz, Ike Ellison, Kelli Otremba, Catie Lawrence, Jim Hollis, and the whole NextGen crew past and present.

For my education in the production of the work: John Tighe, Tim Grahl, Jamie Cohen, Chuck Rockroad, Chris Naish, Ivan Terzic, Dan Roam, and once again Lesley Kontowicz.

Finally, everyone reading this page. A writer is nothing without an audience. I genuinely hope that the things in this book help elevate your success to the highest levels and have the same affect on your life as it has on mine.

Recommended Reading

As a voracious consumer of books I am frequently asked to recommend sales books. My favorites on every subject would be a work unto itself. Here are some of my favorites in the area of sales and sales management.

Sales

Achieve Sales Excellence: The 7 Customer Rules for Becoming the New Sales Professional - Howard Stevens, Theodore Kinni

Adapt or Fail: Process with Power - Michael Nick

Agile Selling: Get Up to Speed Quickly in Today's Ever-Changing Sales World - Jill Konrath

Amp Up Your Sales: Powerful Strategies That Move Customers to Make Fast, Favorable Decisions - Andy Paul

Be Bold and Win the Sale: Get Out of Your Comfort Zone and Boost Your Performance - Jeff Shore

Consultative Selling: The Hanan Formula for High-Margin Sales at High Levels - Mack Hanan

Dealstorming: The Secret Weapon That Can Solve Your Toughest Sales Challenges - Tim Sanders

DISCOVER Questions Get You Connected: for Professional Sellers - Deb Calvert

EDGY Conversations: How Ordinary People Can Achieve Outrageous Success - Dan Waldschmidt

Emotional Intelligence for Sales Success: Connect with Customers and Get Results - Colleen Stanley

Endless Referrals - Bob Burg

Escaping the Price-Driven Sale: How World Class Sellers Create Extraordinary Profit - Tom Snyder, Kevin Kearns

Fanatical Prospecting: The Ultimate Guide to Opening Sales Conversations and Filling the Pipeline by Leveraging Social Selling, Telephone, Email, Text, and Cold Calling - Jeb Blount

Go for No! Yes is the Destination, No is How You Get There - Richard Fenton

Go-Givers Sell More - Bob Burg

High-Profit Selling: Win the Sale Without Compromising on Price - Mark Hunter

How I Raised Myself From Failure to Success in Selling - Frank Bettge

How to Become a Rainmaker: The Rules for Getting and Keeping Customers and Clients - Jeffery J. Fox

Influence: Science and Practice - Robert B. Cialdini

Insight Selling: Surprising Research on What Sales Winners Do Differently - Mike Schultz, John E. Doerr

Integrity Selling for the 21st Century: How to Sell the Way People Want to Buy - Ron Willingham

Jeffrey Gitomer's Little Red Book of Selling: 12.5 Principles for sales greatness: How to make sales FOREVER - Jeffrey Gitomer

Let's Get Real or Let's Not Play: Transforming the Buyer/Seller Relationship - Mahan Khalsa

Love Is the Killer App: How to Win Business and Influence Friends - Tim Sanders

Mastering the Complex Sale - Jeff Thull

New Sales. Simplified.: The Essential Handbook for Prospecting and New Business Development - Mike Weinberg

No More Cold Calling: The Breakthrough System That Will Leave Your Competition in the Dust - Joanne S. Black

Perfect Selling - Linda Richardson

Pick Up the Damn Phone! How People, Not Technology, Seal the Deal - Joanne S. Black

Rainmaking Conversations: Influence, Persuade, and Sell in Any Situation - Mike Schultz, John E. Doerr

ROI Selling: Increasing Revenue, Profit, and Customer Loyalty through the 360 Sales Cycle - Michael Nick

Screen to Selling: How to Increase Sales, Productivity, and Customer Experience with the Latest Technology - Doug Devitre

Selling Fearlessly: A Master Salesman's Secrets For The One-Call-Close Salesperson - Robert Terson

Selling to Big Companies - Jill Konrath

Selling to the C-Suite: What Every Executive Wants You to Know About Successfully Selling to the Top - Stephen J. Bistritz, Nicholas A.C. Read

Shift!: Harness The Trigger Events That Turn Prospects Into Customers - Craig Elias, Tibor Shanto

Six Secrets Of Sales Magnets: Learn what the TOP 5% of all salespeople do and how YOU can do it too - Laura Posey

Smart Calling: Eliminate the Fear, Failure, and Rejection from Cold Calling - Art Sobczak

SNAP Selling: Speed Up Sales and Win More Business with Today's Frazzled Customers - Jill Konrath

SPIN Selling - Neil Rackham

Swim with the Sharks Without Being Eaten Alive - Harvey Mackay

The 25 Sales Habits of Highly Successful Salespeople - Stephen Schiffman

The 7 Habits of Highly Effective People: Powerful Lessons in Personal Change - Stephen R. Covey

The Challenger Customer: Selling to the Hidden Influencer Who Can Multiply Your Results - Brent Adamson, Matthew Dixon, Pat Spenner, Nick Toman

The Challenger Sale: Taking Control of the Customer Conversation - Matthew Dixon, Brent Adamson

The Greatest Salesman in the World - Og Mandino

The Miracle Morning for Salespeople: The Fastest Way to Take Your SELF and Your SALES to the Next Level - Hal Elrod

The New Strategic Selling: The Unique Sales System Proven Successful by the World's Best Companies - Robert B. Miller, Stephen E. Heiman, Tad Tuleja

The Psychology of Selling: Increase Your Sales Faster and Easier Than You Ever Thought Possible - Brian Tracy

The SPIN Selling Fieldbook: Practical Tools, Methods, Exercises, and Resources - Neil Rackham

Think and Grow Rich - Napoleon Hill

Think Like Your Customer: A Winning Strategy to Maximize Sales by Understanding and Influencing How and Why Your Customers Buy - Bill Stinnet

To Sell Is Human: The Surprising Truth About Moving Others - Daniel H. Pink

Trust-Based Selling: Using Customer Focus and Collaboration to Build Long-Term Relationships - Charles H. Green

Unlimited Selling Power: How to Master Hypnotic Skills - Donald Moine

Sales Management

Awesomely Simple: Essential Business Strategies for Turning Ideas Into Action - John Spence

Cracking the Sales Management Code: The Secrets to Measuring and Managing Sales Performance - Jason Jordan, Michelle Vazzana

Predictable Revenue: Turn Your Business Into A Sales Machine With The $100 Million Best Practices Of Salesforce.com - Aaron Ross

Sales Management Simplified : The Straight Truth About Getting Exceptional Results from Your Sales Team - Mike Weinberg

Sales Manager Survival Guide: Lessons from Sales' Front Lines - David Brock

The Sales Acceleration Formula: Using Data, Technology, and Inbound Selling to go from $0 to $100 Million - Mark Roberge

The Sales Development Playbook: Build Repeatable Pipeline and Accelerate Growth with Inside Sales - Trish Bertuzzi

The Ultimate Sales Machine: Turbocharge Your Business with Relentless Focus on 12 Key Strategies - Chet Holmes

James Muir

References

Chapter 1

1. CSO Insights, SiriusDecisions

2. CareerBuilder, www.Careerbuilder.com

3. Huthwaite's white paper, Creating Real Value

4. SPIN Selling - McGraw-Hill Education; 1st edition (May 1, 1988), p.44

5. SPIN Selling - McGraw-Hill Education; 1st edition (May 1, 1988), p.24-37

6. The Speed of Trust: The One Thing That Changes Everything - Free Press 2005, p.13

Chapter 2

1. SPIN Selling - McGraw-Hill Education; 1st edition (May 1, 1988) p.21

2. SPIN Selling - McGraw-Hill Education; 1st edition (May 1, 1988) p.26

3. SPIN Selling - McGraw-Hill Education; 1st edition (May 1, 1988) p.28

4. SPIN Selling - McGraw-Hill Education; 1st edition (May 1, 1988) p.31

5. SPIN Selling - McGraw-Hill Education; 1st edition (May 1, 1988) p.33

6. SPIN Selling - McGraw-Hill Education; 1st edition (May 1, 1988) p.30

7. SPIN Selling - McGraw-Hill Education; 1st edition (May 1, 1988) p.33

8. SPIN Selling - McGraw-Hill Education; 1st edition (May 1, 1988) p.34

9. Do closing techniques diminish prospect trust? - Jon M. Hawes, James T. Strong, Bernard S. Winick - Industrial Marketing Management Volume 25, Issue 5, September 1996, Pages 349–360

10. The Pain of Deciding: Indecision, Flexibility, and Consumer Choice Online - On Amir - Massachusetts Institute of Technology

11. The Hassled Decision Maker: The Effects of Perceived Time Pressure on Information Processing in Decision Making by Leon Mann † Charlotte Tan †

12. Examining the Impact of Life Satisfaction and Time Pressure on Consumers' Responses towards Cause-Related Marketing Promotions - Bobbie YL Chan, The Open University of Hong Kong

13. Testing the boundaries of the choice overload phenomenon: The effect of number of options and time pressure on decision difficulty and satisfaction - Graeme A. Haynes - Article first published online: 9 FEB 2009 - Psychology and Marketing - Special Issue: Assortment Structure and Choice - Volume 26, Issue 3,

pages 204–212, March 2009

14. The Sales Board researched over 350,000 salespeople from a wide variety of industiries and found that 62% of salespeople fail to ask for commitment. http://www.thesalesboard.com

15. Max Sacks International reports that their studies also show that 62% of all sales people never ask for the order. http://www.maxsacks.com

16. William Winston and Joseph P Vaccaro in Managing Sales Professionals, Routledge also report the 60% figure.

17. Jeffery Fox reports that according to their studies 90 percent of salespeople don't ask for the order. http://www.foxandcompany.com/ also Secrets of Great Rainmakers, Hachette Books

18. Mike Stewart, in Close More Sales, AMACOM, reports that 70 percent of buyers report that they are never asked to buy.

19. SPIN Selling - McGraw-Hill Education; 1st edition (May 1, 1988) p.40

20. SPIN Selling - McGraw-Hill Education; 1st edition (May 1, 1988) p.41

21. Research conducted by Sales Benchmark Index, 58% of qualified deals end in no decision. http://www.salesbenchmarkindex.com/

22. Research from CustomerCentric Selling estimates that 60% - 80% of deals are lost to no-decision. http://www.customercentric.com/news-and-resources/articles/failing-to-close

23. Don Linder, the founder of Major Client Selling reports that 40% of deals are lost to no-decision. http://www.majorclients.com/articles/200707lostabigsale.html

24. Research conducted by Wayne M. Thomas author of The Sales Manager's Success Manual, AMACOM, suggests that 55% of deals are lost to no-decision.

25. The Distribution of MBTI Type In General Population, Allen Hammer and Wayne Mitchell, CPP, Inc. Study of normative sample of 1267 adults, Journal of Psychological Type, Volume 37, 1996

26. Selling with Noble Purpose: How to Drive Revenue and Do Work That Makes You Proud Hardcover – Wiley, by Lisa Earle McLeod

Chapter 3

1. A. Freitas-Magalhães, Microexpression and macroexpression, Encyclopedia of Human Behavior (Vol. 2, pp.173-183). Oxford: Elsevier/Academic Press.

2. Paul Ekman, Emotions Revealed. New York: Henry Holt and Co.

3. Paul Ekman Group - http://www.paulekman.com/micro-expressions/

4. Nick Morgan, Power Cues, p.119

5. Van Berkum, J.J., Van den Brink, D., Tesink, C.M., Kos, M., & Hagoort, P. (2008). The neural integration of speaker and message. Journal of Cognitive Neuroscience, 20, 580–591.

6. Visual and paralinguistic cues, confidence, and perceived trustworthiness - 2012 - Tsankova, E; Möllering, G; Kappas, A; Krumhuber, E; Aubrey, A; Manstead, A; Marshall, D; (2012) Visual and paralinguistic cues, confidence, and perceived trustworthiness. In: Castaldo, S and Ferrin, D and Möllering, G and Priem, R and Skinner, D and Weibel, A and Zolin, R, (eds.) Proceedings of the 6th Workshop on Trust Within and Between Organizations. (pp. 1 - 15). : Milan, Italy.

7. Meltzoff, A.N. (1995). "Understanding the intentions of others: Re-enactment of intended acts by 18-month-old children". *Developmental Psychology* **31** (5): 838–850

8. Meltzoff, A.N.; Brooks, R. (2001). ""Like me" as a building block for understanding other minds: Bodily acts, attention, and intention". In Malle, B.F.; Moses, L.J.; Baldwin, D.A. *Intentions and intentionality: Foundations of social cognition*. Cambridge, MA: MIT Press. pp. 171–191.

9. Wojciszke, B. et al. (1998) On the dominance of moral categories in impression formation. Pers. Soc. Psychol. Bull. 24, 1245–1257

10. Susan T. Fiske. et al. (2006) Universal dimensions of social cognition: warmth and competence. Trends in Cognitive Sciences Vol.11 No.2

11. Cacioppo, J.T. et al. (1997) Beyond bipolar conceptualizations and measures: the case of attitudes and evaluative space. Pers. Soc. Psychol. Rev. 1, 3–25

12. Peeters, G. (2001) From good and bad to can and must: subjec-

tive necessity of acts associated with positively and negatively valued stimuli. Eur. J. Soc. Psychol. 31, 125–136

13. Reeder, G.D. et al. (2002) Inferences about the morality of an aggressor: the role of perceived motive. J. Pers. Soc. Psychol. 83, 789–803

14. Reeder, G.D. et al. (2002) Inferences about the morality of an aggressor: the role of perceived motive. J. Pers. Soc. Psychol. 83, 789–803

15. I want to honor author and mentor Mahan Khalsa for sparking this realization in myself. You can read his work in Let's Get Real or Let's Not Play has : Transforming the Buyer/Seller Relationship by Mahan Khalsa (Author), Randy Illig (Author), Stephen R. Covey (Introduction)

16. Emotion precedes body language and conscious thought. http://en.wikipedia.org/wiki/Cannon%E2%80%93Bard_theory

17. "Boost Power Through Body Language". HBR Blog Network. Harvard Business Review. Retrieved 28 May 2012. Carney, Dana R.; Cuddy, Amy J. C.; Yap, Andy J. (October 2010).

18. "Power Posing – Brief Nonverbal Displays Affect Neuroendocrine Levels and Risk Tolerance". Journal of the Association for Psychological Science 21 (10): 1363–1368. doi:10.1177/0956797610383437. PMID 20855902.

19. Venton, Danielle (15 May 2012). "Power Postures Can Make You Feel More Powerful". Wired. Retrieved 28 May 2012.

20. Halverson, Ph.D., Heidi Grant. "Feeling Timid and Powerless?

Maybe It's How You Are Sitting". The Science of Success. Psychology Today. Retrieved 28 May 2012.

21. Halverson, Ph.D., Heidi Grant. "Feeling Timid and Powerless? Maybe It's How You Are Sitting". The Science of Success. Psychology Today. Retrieved 28 May 2012

22. Perspectives on Psychological Science July 2011 vol. 6 no. 4 348-356 Antonis Hatzigeorgiadis⇓, Nikos Zourbanos, Evangelos Galanis, Yiannis Theodorakis

23. Baker, S. B., E. Johnson, M. Kopala, and N. J. Strout. (September 1985). "Test Interpretation Competence: A Comparison of Microskills and Mental Practice Training." Counselor Education and Supervision 25: 31-43.

24. Swanson, H. L., and E. B. Kozleski. (July 1985). "Self-Talk and Handicapped Children's Academic Needs: Applications of Cognitive Behavior Modification." Techniques: A Journal For Remedial Education and Counseling 1: 367-379, 115-125.

25. Steffy, R. A., D. Meichenbaum, and J. A. Best. (1970). "Aversive and Cognitive Factors in the Modification of Smoking Behavior." Behavioral Research and Therapy 8: 115-125.

26. Burns, D. (1980). Feeling Good: The New Mood Therapy. New York: William Morrow.

27. Ellis, A. (1977). The Basic Clinical Theory of Rational-Emotive Therapy. New York: Springer.

Chapter 4

1. Sales Behaviour links to Sales Success By Professor Lynette Ryals and Dr Iain Davies, Thank:Cranfield – 2011

2. Key account planning: benefits, barriers and best practice, Lynette Ryals and Beth Rogers, Journal of Strategic Marketing Volume 15, Issue 2-3, 2007

3. Sources of effectiveness in the business-to-business sales organization - Nigel F. Piercy, Cardiff Business School; David W. Cravens, Texas Christian University and Neil A. Morgan, University of Cambridge. Journal of Marketing Practice: Applied Marketing Science, Vol. 3 No. 1, 1997, pp. 43-69. © MCB University Press, 1355-2538

4. Niel Rackham The SPIN Selling Fieldbook, 1996 p. 3.

Chapter 5

1. Fazio, Blascovich & Driscoll, 1992) Fazio, R.H., Blascovich, J., & Driscoll, D. (1992) On the functional value of attitudes. Personality and Social Psychology Bulletin, 18, 388-401.

2. (Cialdini, 2001) Robert Cialdini Influence: Science and Practice, p82.

3. Nunes, J. C. and Dreze, X. (2006). The endowed progress effect: how artificial advancement increases effort. Journal of Consumer Research. 32, 504-512.

Chapter 6

No References

Chapter 7

No References

Chapter 8

No References

Chapter 9

1. Gartner Research, 2014

2. Corporate Executive Board (CEB), MLC Customer Purchase Research Survey, 2011.

3. Customer Experience Diagnostic; CEB Sales Leadership Council research 2014, HR Chally World Class Sales Research 1992-2016

4. Susan Mulcahy – "Evaluating the costs of sales calls in business to business markets: a study of more than 23,000 business" (Washington: Cahners Research, January 2002), p.8

5. Escaping the Price-Driven Sale, Tom Snyder and Kevin Kearns

Chapter 10

1. Sales Behaviour links to Sales Success By Professor Lynette Ryals and Dr Iain Davies, Thank:Cranfield – 2011

2. Key account planning: benefits, barriers and best practice, Lynette Ryals and Beth Rogers, Journal of Strategic Marketing Volume 15, Issue 2-3, 2007

3. Sources of effectiveness in the business-to-business sales organization - Nigel F. Piercy, Cardiff Business School; David W. Cravens,

Texas Christian University and Neil A. Morgan, University of Cambridge. Journal of Marketing Practice: Applied Marketing Science, Vol. 3 No. 1, 1997, pp. 43-69. © MCB University Press, 1355-2538

4. Niel Rackham The SPIN Selling Fieldbook, 1996 p. 3.

Chapter 11

No references.

Chapter 12

No References

Chapter 13

No References

Index

Giacomo Rizzolatti, 28

Goal, 25-26, 37, 43, 45-48, 59, 64-66, 69, 71, 75-76, 97, 104, 124, 126, 144-145, 162, 165, 175-177, 202

Group, 45, 48, 64, 90, 95, 98-99, 101, 132, 165, 172, 187, 206-207, 242

Guide, 8, 11, 25, 125, 170, 172, 175, 194, 234, 237

Happiness, 29, 44, 59-60, 228

Helpful, 38-39, 89, 95, 106, 128, 137, 163, 172, 180, 198, 206-207, 209, 212, 229

Helpfulness, 33-34, 37-38, 40, 42

Helping, 10, 19, 23, 26, 76, 149

Helps, 92, 120, 164, 167, 180, 220

High-Value Questions, 131, 133-134, 148, 220

Homework, 93, 144, 207

Hope, 37, 50, 70, 165, 171, 186, 228, 231

Human, 29-30, 84, 106, 237, 242

Huthwaite, 21, 118-119, 126, 142, 239

Hypothesis, 51, 147

Idea, 3, 14, 19, 39, 47, 51, 65, 94, 98, 100, 103, 115, 128, 135-137, 139, 149, 172, 181, 206, 237

Ideal advance, 76, 87-88, 99-100, 103-104, 148-149, 162, 173, 175-176, 185, 200, 204, 207, 216-217, 220-221

Identified, 33, 117, 119, 124, 126

Identify, 9, 44, 58, 99, 124, 127, 137, 164, 170, 220

Illustrate, 56, 73, 90, 115, 195

Immediately, 32, 60-61, 71, 83-84, 180, 187, 194, 196, 228

Impact, 32, 83-84, 99, 106-107, 124, 127, 145, 160, 179, 188, 193, 218, 227, 240

Importance, 37, 109, 145, 161, 163-164

Impossible, 30, 50, 90, 106, 185, 188, 229

Impression, 31, 42, 184, 243

Improve, 14, 32, 38-39, 41-42, 44, 59-60, 65, 67, 75-77, 81, 83, 103, 128, 141, 160-161, 165, 176-177, 180, 185, 198, 228

Improved, 17, 46, 61, 101, 137

Improvement, 25, 60, 146, 175, 199

Improving, 8, 61, 66-67, 166

Incremental, 69, 88

Indicator, 23, 61-62, 92, 96, 147, 185-186

Individual, 2, 7, 15, 29, 31, 46-47, 52, 58, 76, 117, 129, 133, 165, 168-169, 189, 194, 209, 216, 229

Industry, 1-2, 21-22, 82, 106, 113, 119, 138, 145, 149, 213, 221

Inexperienced, 9, 121, 180, 186, 193-194

Influence, 65, 74, 107-108, 133, 177, 234-235, 246

Information, 2, 9, 30, 38-39, 57, 59-60, 64, 79, 93, 95-96, 105-107, 109, 113-114, 116-118, 129, 132, 138, 142, 144, 147-148, 156, 169, 184, 192, 220, 227-228, 240

Ingenious, 90, 100

About James Muir

James Muir is the author of *The Perfect Close: The Secret to Closing Sales - The Best Selling Practices & Techniques for Closing the Deal* that shows sales and service professionals a clear, practical, and comfortable approach that will increase their number of closed opportunities and accelerate their sales to the highest levels while remaining genuinely, authentic.

James is a professional sales trainer, author, speaker and coach. He has shattered records as both a field rep and manager. His guidance comes from the school of hard knocks. Three decades of experience has given James a fresh and practical perspective on what works in real life and what doesn't.

James has an extensive background in healthcare where he has sold and spoken to the largest names in technology and healthcare including HCA, Tenet, Catholic Healthcare, Banner, Dell, IBM, and others.

Focused on helping individuals and teams improve and streamline their business practices, James covers a variety of today's most important topics, including: closing, productivity, management, lead generation, sales strategies, and authentic sales skills.

Those interested in learning a more can reach him at PureMuir.com.

Contact Info

Phone: 801-633-4444

Website: PureMuir.com

Email: jmuir @ PureMuir.com

LinkedIn: https://www.linkedin.com/in/puremuir

Twitter: @B2B_SalesTips

Made in the USA
San Bernardino, CA
02 March 2018